# Shot Through The Heart

Blessings + Love,
Linda Porter

# ALSO BY LINDA PORTER

*Angels, Beings of Light—The Wisdom and Teachings of God's Messengers on Earth*

# Shot Through The Heart
## or
### How God Uses Love to Open Us Up to the Divine and Each Other

# Linda Porter and Us

iUniverse, Inc.

New York  Bloomington  Shanghai

# Shot Through The Heart
## or How God Uses Love to Open Us Up to the Divine and Each Other

iUniverse books may be ordered through booksellers or by contacting:

iUniverse
1663 Liberty Drive
Bloomington, IN 47403
www.iuniverse.com
1-800-Authors (1-800-288-4677)

Because of the dynamic nature of the Internet, any Web addresses or links contained in this book may have changed since publication and may no longer be valid.

The views expressed in this work are solely those of the author and do not necessarily reflect the views of the publisher, and the publisher hereby disclaims any responsibility for them.

First 3 paragraphs from page 16, used as epigraph, from WARRIOR OF THE LIGHT: A MANUAL by PAULO COELHO Copyright © 2003 by Paulo Coelho. Reprinted by permission of HarperCollins Publishers

ISBN: 978-0-595-50967-6 (pbk)
ISBN: 978-0-595-61713-5 (ebk)

Printed in the United States of America

To *Mick St. John,* the fictional vampire in the CBS television series *Moonlight,* who caused me to absorb what I already knew—that the Light can be found in anyone and everyone—even in those whom others deem to personify darkness.

And to all of you who have asked for more words, I thank you, and have done my best to honor your request.

*The moment that he [she] begins to walk along it,*
*the Warrior of the Light recognizes the Path.*
*Each stone, each bend cries welcome to him [her].*
*He [She] identifies with the mountains and the streams,*
*he [she] sees something of his [her] own soul in the plants*
*and the animals and the birds of the field.*
*Then, accepting the help of God*
*and of God's Signs,*
*he [she] allows his [her] Personal Legend to guide him [her]*
*toward the tasks that life has reserved for him [her].*

from *The Warrior of the Light*
by Paulo Coelho

# CONTENTS

# WORDS OF GRATITUDE

A book is not made, nor a life lived, in a vacuum. The following have all been important to both endeavors and to them I give my heartfelt gratitude:

First and foremost, I wish to thank my husband, Dr. John Porter. He acted as a sounding board and consultant, but what I treasure most is his acceptance of who and what I have become. His support and encouragement during this phase has made him my anchor in the sometimes turbulent seas that occur as one deliberately walks a spiritual path. Besides being a skillful physical healer (an anesthesiologist), John has an ability to soothe and comfort his patients that goes beyond anything that can be taught. The Light expresses itself in many forms.

To my sons, Mathew and Alex Porter—*Mom* has always been, and will always be, my most important job description. Without our mutual love and respect, my life would not seem so bright. Both of them have helped in numerous ways, including formatting and technical expertise. Each has also shared their artistic skills and creativity. Thanks to Mathew for this awesome book cover. It is beyond anything I could have imagined. Thanks to Alex for the delicious web-site. He managed to capture exactly what I needed, and much more, including the blog which was totally his idea. I am so proud of them both.

To my granddaughter, London Porter, whose light is amazing in one so young. I know, without a doubt, that her brightness will continue to grow, illuminating everyone and everything she comes in contact with.

To Beth, Samantha, and Cameron, who are about to become official members of our family, but have already touched our hearts as such.

To my mother and stepfather, Alice and Don Baker and my mother-in-law and father-in-law, Victor and Kristine Porter, and the rest of my extended family. The love and support of family can not be overrated. I have been blessed with one of the best.

To my dear friend, Vicky Freeman, who is always there to share the revelations of my journey and often is a participant in the exploits—a willing one, of course.

To the congregation of First United Methodist Church of South Bend, Indiana. They are the most loving, open, and accepting people I could ever imagine. This church is a place where the sages and the seekers co-mingle to form such a whole that an atmosphere of love always prevails. Truly divine.

To my pastor, Reverend Mary Hubbard, whose acceptance and encouragement brought hope to dispel the wariness. She was instrumental in helping me to see that it was time to let my light shine again.

To the United Methodist Women, who envelop everything they do in love. Their support and encouragement continues to "blow me away." Thank you!

To the workers of the First United Methodist Church Soup Kitchen. From the paid help to the many volunteers, these people willingly give of their time to give nourishment to others. They not only hand out food but love, as well. Words can not express my joy in being able to work with them in such a labor of love.

To Susan Jebelian, Juliann Jebelian, and Lyndsey Borst, who help me take care of my house so that I am free to indulge in the wanderings that constantly beckon me.

To the staff at SALON ROUGE, especially Kelly Johnson, Ronda Ward, and Peggie O'Neill, who work at beautifying my outside as I try to work on the inside.

To the other women in my *sisterhood*, including Rhonda Biritz, Diana Green, Patti McCready, Mary Welsheimer, Genelle King, Bev Gramza, Sally Zablocki, Deb Farmer, Jean Hugus, Nila Howell, Miriam Olson, and Yvonne Walker. There are also many more, too numerous to mention. I could write a book just on all the women who have impacted me deeply.

Then there are three special men: Ike Lash, Floyd Hugus, and Jon Freeman. Obviously, they can not be included in the sisterhood, but they continue to give me such support and encouragement that they deserve much thanks.

To Paulo Coelho, who manages to entertain and enlighten at the same time. I knew his work had impacted me, but I had no idea how much until I was in the midst of this book. I wish him all the best and hope that he continues his important work well into the future.

And to all of the *Moonlight* fans out there who have bonded into communities. You are all amazing and I consider it a privilege to be one of you. Your loving, passionate, and yes, intense energy has often made my day. You have filled me with fun, excitement, passion, and humility. Together, we have worked hard to be certain that such a show, with so much to give, will continue on. But even beyond that, *Moonlight* has inspired us to make the world a better place. Who would ever have imagined that a television show about a vampire would result in a blood and fund drive to benefit the American Red Cross? To me, that is perfection!

Finally, how do I thank God, the Divine, the Source—and the angels that mean so much to me? There are no worldly words to describe my feelings. So, I'll just invite them to listen to my heart. In doing that they'll know without a doubt.

# INTRODUCTION

## *January 2008*

What you hold in your hands is a chronicle. You might even think of it as a journal or something similar to a blog, compiled into book form. It contains entries, writings, of actual events of my life. Most of the events have occurred in the last few months. The others have been added to give clarification or to spice up the tale. All of them are true and written from my perspective. The entire chronicle pertains to the spiritual path I have been aware of walking, and sometimes running, for most of the last decade.

My motive for writing this includes several components; together they have caused this book into being:

- I love to read of the spiritual experiences of others. Most are wonderful and quite amazing. They almost always make a difference in my life.

- I hope that there is something in my story that will be of help to you as you travel your own spiritual path.

- Probably the most important reason is that I was told by *angels* to write my experiences down and create a book.

- The most deeply felt reason is that I wanted to immortalize this period of my life, one that has impacted me so deeply.

Perhaps the underlying goal is to encourage you to be open to such incredible adventures as I have experienced, to know the love that I have encountered. If I have helped, in even a small way, then I will be happy. Actually, I can be happy anyway. That's the beauty of it all.

I suppose I should tell you this: I converse with *angels*. That's right—*angels*. I explained all of that in my first book, *Angels: Beings of Light*. In order for this book to make sense, you need to know that. Whether you believe it is up to you.

One more thing: In my desire to produce the best quality book I could, I consulted a professional editor. She recommended that I leave the book as it is and "let it fly." She felt that it would be a mistake to tamper with the mystical and even my expressions of such experiences. I treasure her honesty and her understanding. In my heart, I know she is right. I don't have the ability to bring you a perfect book, but I do have the ability to bring you a perfect message—a message of *Love*. So, I give our words to you, "as is," realizing that they are perfect in their imperfection.

# RESOLVING THE PAST

Truthfully, I didn't know if I would ever write again, at least for anyone else's eyes. It was as if I had lost my magic. I knew it wasn't magic, of course, but that's what it felt like to me. Maybe I needed the rest. Or maybe it was self-imposed exile. Maybe it was to lick my wounds. Or maybe it was just that I needed time to grow, to experience more, to live and learn before I would have anything more to say.

I could see it in the eyes of others—the disappointment, the wondering why I'd lost it. What answers could I give as to why I was no longer writing in any significant way? How could someone lose that incredible connection? What had she done to cause the angels to become silent, or as good as silent? My inner vitality was gone. It wasn't that my life stopped. Everything went on as before. Life was lived, of course—a very happy and fulfilling life, and I was better equipped to live it than ever before. It wasn't that I doubted what was there, what was available to tap into as we stumble through this life. It wasn't that I forgot. It wasn't that I felt alone to do earthly battles all by myself. It wasn't like that. It was just that I no longer felt the need, except on occasion. I'd lost the spark of connection.

The angels allowed me that. They rarely spoke unless I asked, and I asked less and less. I, of all people, put it aside and went on with my life.

It wasn't that I'd lost my connection to God. My awareness of that special connection remained strong, even grew. I was a believer. My trust in God never faltered and I continued to allow myself to be used—to be a conduit for God's love. All through the desert times my devotion never lessened.

So perhaps this time *away* was always part of the plan, but it was I who enforced it. Why? Perhaps I no longer trusted myself and my abilities. Perhaps I no longer thought I had anything else to give. Perhaps I chose to believe that such a magical time was limited and that I'd had my time in the sun. Perhaps I thought I had fulfilled my *obligation* and nothing more would be required of me. My *job* was done. Maybe I hadn't even done a good job with what I was given.

The reasons were multi-fold, as they always are. On a purely pragmatic side, I discovered I didn't like the business end of book selling. It made me extremely uncomfortable—like selling myself. I suspect the larger reason was that I allowed myself to be affected by the disapproval of those I had placed in authority of myself. How silly. I should have known better—did know better—but couldn't seem to muster the ability to move beyond the hurt and dismay.

And then, of course, there was the Iraq War. I had written predictions about hope and love, but now, there was such division among people; frustration, anger, and vitriol unlike anything I had ever encountered. Where was that longed for love, that expectation of wonder that I had anticipated and perhaps had led others to believe in? I didn't know what to do with those feelings of disappointment, and I'm just going to say it—*shame.* Perhaps it was as simple as being told of a future not so distant. Much beauty and love was shown following September 11, 2001. We came together as a people to care, to mourn, to love. Of course, the ending has not yet been reached. The possibility exists that the situation may turn around or maybe the extreme negativity that has engulfed us for so long has taken its toll. Is it possible that the energy that we send out as a whole has set into motion a measure of aggression and violence that was unforeseen by me? Regardless, I have long known that we can't accurately judge something as a blessing or a curse until it plays out, and even then it's just the label we give—a story we tell about it.

Does God allow us the freedom to determine the outcome? Do our actions and choices have more to do with what happens than we realize? If that is true, then perhaps it's time that we all put more love out there, even love for our perceived enemy. I'm not just referring to the other side in an armed conflict. That's an easy example and even that is difficult to define. War comes in many guises. How do we show love, for whom do we show love, and how do we deal with the violent intent in others are, no doubt, questions for the ages. What about the warring we do as individuals with those we fiercely disagree with; those we want to change, that we feel it's our responsibility to change? What about the war that goes on inside ourselves; the violent words and actions we use to try to cause us to change, maybe even conform; the words that tear us down instead of lovingly build us up? I know how I'm choosing to use the charge in my own life. I have learned much about love and hate and how it affects us. Trust me, I'd prefer to take love every time.

As I look back, I am beginning to realize that things had not been as stagnant as they seemed. Events were set into motion that would bring me to this time, this space, this place. Nothing was lost during my perceived sojourn in the desert. I was living and learning and growing—evolving, if you will. Yes, *divine guidance* is a wonderful thing, connecting with energies on other levels. It brings vibrancy to life and also contains an inordinate amount of help. It even helps smooth out the rough edges of day to day living. I had already conveyed that in my first book. More information was not necessary. My path now contained elements that were richer and deeper, for I needed to take the next step of the journey. What I didn't realize was that once I had begun it, there was no looking back. The past had fulfilled itself, and what awaited in my future would take me to other places, other experiences, other passions. If only I had known.

# IN THE BEGINNING

*A Vampire Loving Female Warrior of Light that just happens to be me—that is what you want me to write about?!* I'm sure the panic in me could have been felt around the neighborhood. *Oh, yeah. They're really going to love this one. What happened to the lovely, flowery, non-controversial (Didn't I say non-controversial?) book of sweetness and light that I thought we were going to write? You know, the one about opening your heart space. What happened to Heartspeake?* I knew, of course. I just wasn't ready to give in so easily. Sometimes I have to do a little wrestling with the angels; maybe it's just to pass the time, to give me time to absorb what I already know to be true. Because feelings (heart feelings) show me the knowing; whether I am ready to admit it intellectually is another matter. And both sides enter into the negotiations knowing that they always prevail. Every single time.

That was not the only thing about this project that shocked me. I was shocked time and time again. This book is nothing like what I envisioned when we began. However, opening your heart space is the dominant theme; at least I think it is. Perhaps it's the thinking that gets me into trouble. More likely it's the thinking combined with the feeling that gives me the balance I need.

We were about ten days into the book when it began to occur to me that this book was not shaping up to be the book I had anticipated. It was another couple of days until I acknowledged that what we were producing was the book it was always meant to be.

In between came the title. Ah, what to say about the title? For my last book, *Angels: Beings of Light—The Wisdom and Teachings of God's Messengers on Earth,* the title came to me during that lovely time between sleeping and awakening. That's a time, along with cleansing with water (taking a shower, brushing my teeth, washing my face), that I seem to be exceptionally open to *otherworldly perceptions.* This time I had picked up the word *Heartspeake* from an angel writing describing what I call the mandate for this book. I loved the word; it flowed off your tongue. It had an ancient feel to it. I wanted it to be the title. I called it the working title. Obviously I was aware that it wasn't the title no matter how much I wanted it to be. But it was a good run. For a few days I was writing a lovely book called *Heartspeake.* The fact that I was also writing about vampires didn't seem incongruous to me. Welcome to my life.

The weekend began with my husband, John, throwing out ideas for the title. Nothing felt quite right. Besides, it was *Heartspeake,* wasn't it? I was just waiting for confirmation. On Saturday morning he came up with even more. Still the same—nothing felt quite right. I told him I thought I needed something a little edgier (the insights were beginning to take hold) and I also reminded him how the last title came to me. I recognized it the moment it appeared. I assumed this would come to me the same way, but assumptions can cause unneeded distress. I know that and I try to let things flow, not always successfully. John was on his way out the door to breakfast when it came to me—the title. Even though I recognized it immediately, I was stunned! I ran down the stairs to try to catch him before he left, but I was too late. I ran back upstairs and just stood there in disbelief, *all the while believing.* All I could hear was Bon Jovi singing about being shot through the heart and giving love a bad name. That mind connection didn't bode well for the book title. I immediately sent an e-mail to my son, Alex. The subject—Please Tell Me This Isn't The Book Title!! His response was the best ever—*I do love the title, I think.* Precisely.

I then headed off to the United Methodist Women's Christmas Brunch. I know they could sense a little angst, a little edge to my demeanor. I told them I had some wrestling with angels to do. They know me quite well. Being with them was the best possible place I could be, sharing friendship, food, and Christmas music. A whole lotta' love went on there; love that I needed and received.

When I returned home, John was out raking leaves. I took a deep breath and shared with him the new title, the true title of the book.

To my surprise, he liked it and began explaining that there are actual medical procedures which involve putting holes in the heart. (He is a physician, an anesthesiologist.) He told me about a medical technique called transmyocardial laser revascularization. In this procedure, a laser is used to shoot holes through the heart wall. Strangely enough, this seemingly destructive medical technique, in many cases, helps heal otherwise blood starved heart muscle. John also explained that there are times, when a heart has stopped beating, that epinephrine is injected directly into the heart to restart a viable cardiac rhythm.

A shot in the heart can be healing. So, being shot through the heart with love by God … Wow!

As I began to live with this title, taking it in, feeling it, I began to suspect there was more to it than you could see on the surface. I think it has it's own agenda. One that teaches us about releasing judgments, dissolving boundaries, and recognizing that labels can be useless when it comes to spiritual concepts.

And so I give you:

*Shot Through The Heart*
*or*
*How God Uses Love to Open Us Up to the Divine and Each Other*

Enjoy! Indulge! And Learn!

# WRESTLING WITH ANGELS

In the previous entry I wrote about sometimes engaging in wrestling with angels. I would like to share with you the very example I was referring to at that time. It concerns the title of the book.

"Is there any point in discussing what I think you have given me as a title for the book?"

*Shot Through The Heart*
*or*
*How God Uses Love to Open Us Up to the Divine and Each Other*

*Of course there is always a point to discussing anything that worries you or makes you uncomfortable. We do not put things out there deliberately to shake you up. However, we do enjoy your reactions. We put things out there to you because they are the best ways to do what needs to be done, and we know that you will realize that as time goes on.*

*Even John liked the title and brought in some beautiful examples. For he caused you to see the healing aspects of such a phrase—healing to the heart, making one more alive. What could be a better example than that?*

*So we urge you to go with it. It will get attention, yes, and is a better fit for what you are writing about this time, and you will not be thought badly of by many. Most will find it intriguing. And many will find you intriguing and that will be good for business—the job at hand.*

*We do not (nor does God) ever fault you for wanting to discuss or confirm, and we recognize that some things we give you feel so shocking at first that you must stress some and work through that. But we see what you do not and we know what you are capable of. So know that we work with you in love and love only and there is not really any need to fear.*

*But if your question is: Is this the title for your book? You bet! And by the way, it will be a beautiful book full of love and light and will speak to many hearts. See—therein lies the heartspeake. It's all still there. Only the name has been changed to protect the innocent. Ha Ha. Us*

As you can see, wrestling with angels is a fairly peaceful exercise. They always win, but they do it with such love that I can't resist an occasional bout.

# SPEAKING FROM THE HEART

This book has definitely been more difficult to write than the first one. In *Angels: Beings of Light*, I was responsible for the telling of my story, of how my search for God resulted in a spiritual awakening that included a relationship with a group of angels who were guiding and protecting me. They, in turn, gave me teachings on various spiritual topics. Of course, there was the matter of interpreting their communications, the translating into words on a page. That was the easy part.

It soon became apparent this book was to be more about me and less about them. That was disconcerting. I thought the whole point was to make you aware of them, to help you realize that you all have help and protection to turn to. Instead, I was to write about my spiritual journey, with them providing the commentary. More about me? What could I possibly have to write about that would make an interesting book, let alone fill a book? Of course I began questioning. That is what I do.

"What do I do? I don't want to take any credit from you. I don't want this to become an ego thing on my part. You are so responsible for where I am—who I am."

> Linda,
> This is not about us; it is about you. This is more chronicle of Your spiritual journey. It's your path. You are the Warrior. We walk the path with you as protectors and

*guides. But you Choose where to walk, when to walk, if to walk, and what to make of the signs along the way. Never fear. You will give credit where credit is due. We are in this together. One for All and All for One. You have our blessings on this project—one of beauty, goodness, love, life, and trust. You wear it well. Us*

In the very telling of my spiritual journey, this book is more feeling oriented. It is about concepts difficult to grasp, to hold onto, to put into words. There are many ways that our paths to God manifest and usually there is some overlapping. However, each path seems to contain one dominant theme. I have long known that my way is through the heart. Try describing concepts like feelings, light, magic, passion, love, or speaking and listening through the heart. Everything I attempt to write seems so hard to describe, like I am at a loss for words, like there are no words for what I am attempting to portray. And everyone has his or her own interpretation of what a word means. How can I write this in a way that results in understanding?

*Linda, Precious One,*

*We realize what we have asked is a more difficult journey—the attempt to put feelings into words. But don't you realize that is what you do all the time—your feelings always show through the words you are using—through your conversation. Even when you are not talking, your feelings are on display for anyone who is observing. You always speak from your heart. So no matter the words you use, others will pick up on what you are trying to convey. In this case you are speaking heart to heart. It is a different kind of communication. But it will affect others and yourself on a much deeper level than at first noticed on the surface. Oh, yes, there will be surface communication and that will be pleasant and rewarding, but the deeper level, the darker level, will make more of the impact you are hoping for. You are about teaching others to open their heart space—to allow God in just a tiny bit more—to trust in the goodness and the beauty and the love that can only reside there. Where your treasure is, there will your heart be also. Teach them to value their heart and their heartspeake. Show them the beauty of allowing that part to take a prominent place in their lives. Allow them to know that it is not always easy—that placing such value on your heart space makes you vulnerable. Allow them to know that when that space opens wider and wider you are open to more love and beauty than they can imagine, but that also makes you more fragile. You are now open to more possibilities of hurt, of fear. The depth of the feelings intensify. Show them that fear need not rule. Show them how wonderful those moments of passionate grace are. You can do this. You live it. Just show them. Attempt to describe but just show. That is your way. Us*

Obviously, they are a lot more eloquent than I am. Great. I just love being told to allow myself to be vulnerable to anyone and everyone. The fact is, there have been many times on this journey, that were it not for the trust I held on tightly to, this part of my life could have been destroyed.

Soon after this message came through I was on the web looking up the word heartspeake. If I needed confirmation, this was it:

The following came from a blog called Cerridwen's Cauldron dated November 28, 2006. This is obviously a Wiccan site. I read "… *that you speak from the heart, you are real/honest/raw/and you hold nothing back and this 'heartspeake' comes through your writings.*" This works for me; is it confirmation enough for you?

So there you have it. I received my mandate to write more about myself and my spiritual journey, all the while speaking from my heart. But there will be plenty of commentary from the angels. I have re-opened the floodgates. Their words are flowing again.

# *VAMPIRES AS A PATH TO GOD*

Okay. (Deep breath.) What can I possibly say to explain my connection to a vampire, a fictional one, of course? We all know vampires don't exist. So, before you close the book and run screaming from the room, please read on. I promise you there is no darkness in this—only love and light, and perhaps some acceptance.

On September 28, 2007, vampires came into my life. Seriously—very seriously.

I will freely admit I love television and Friday nights on CBS are the best. Can you imagine me being drawn to a show about a woman who can see ghosts and helps them to go to the Light? How far-fetched is that?

Thanks to my sons, I am a fanatic about the joys of TiVo. As I was watching *Ghost Whisperer*, I was intrigued by the previews for a new show premiering afterwards—*Moonlight*—about a modern day vampire. However, since I was watching later than the original airtime, I realized I had missed it. Not one to be dissuaded, I went online to try to find the episode to watch via computer. Imagine my surprise when I read that CBS was airing it again the next night. I had never heard of a major network replaying an episode so soon, but that is exactly what happened. From the first moment of the show I was hooked.

You need to understand, that except for Dark Shadows, I have never been into vampires in any form, including literature or movies. One Anne Rice novel and movie was enough for me. Actually, I tried to avoid anything having to do with them. As a serious adult I tried to stay vampire free. Everyone knows how dark they are.

But vampires began entering my consciousness big time. Aside from watching *Moonlight* every week (okay, maybe more than once each week), references to vampires were showing up everywhere. The signs were occurring as frequently as those for angels and the Divine Feminine had in the past. Here are some examples:

John had left some sheet music on our piano weeks before, but I had never given any attention to it. One day, as I was walking past, I noticed the title. It was *My Immortal* by *Evanescence*. I sat down to play it and then turned it over. On the other side was written *Dark Shadows*. During a phone conversation with John, he mentioned the salt content of blood. That was not a typical conversation for us, I can assure you. I checked out a *Moonlight* forum on the Internet where I read about a series of vampire books. The title of the first book in the series was *Twilight*. I was typing an e-mail for John; stuffed under his computer keyboard was a hymn, of which the first word was *Immortal*. I then glanced up at the screen where the word *Twilight* stood out in bold black. I later found out that *Twilight* was the original name for the television series that became *Moonlight*. My son, Mathew, sent me an e-mail that said he was dressing as a vampire for Halloween. That was totally out of character for him! You need to be aware that all of this was occurring in a very short period of time, without anyone but my son, Alex, knowing of my growing connection to vampires. I was totally amazed, but also confused, as to what was going on. And the signs continued. I was getting a manicure when my nail tech happened to mention a new line of clothing by Sara Jessica Parker, *Bitten*. Even the Dalai Lama spoke of letting a mosquito suck his blood when he is in a good mood! Then there was the billboard advertising the blood bank, showing bags of blood just like the ones *Mick St. John*, of *Moonlight*, uses for his nourishment, and the bottle of Chanel nail polish, *Vamp*.

Separately, these are all fairly common events, but together they form a pattern that I recognize. When I am bombarded with so many connected events, especially in a short period of time, I understand the message. Well, I understand the subject of the message, the meaning, I'm left to discover.

I decided the first thing to do was look into the symbolism of vampires. Perhaps there was something there that would give me a clue as to what was going on. Most of what I read didn't speak to me at all, but then I came upon something that did. I found that there are three meaningful traits that appeal to those who view vampires in a positive way: their strength; their knowledge; and their function as a protective guide. I found this to be very intriguing. I felt like this was the very information I was meant do discover.

By November, it was time to consult the experts. Here is my first conversation regarding the ever-expanding presence of vampires in my life:

11.03.07
"I don't know what to do with all of this—all of the emotions, the questions, the passions."

> *Explore them. See where they take you. We promise you a wild ride but a safe and loving journey. No, no one gets hurt. This is all for you—all for one. Do not be afraid of this. Do not feel you are being neglectful because you are spending time indulging yourself. Yes, this is for you. But when that is true, others benefit. Enjoy. Indulge. And Learn. We said it once. We'll say it again. Here's to you, Little One. Onward and Upward.*

The questioning continued:

11.06.07
"Okay—I don't understand what any of this means. It's like an obsession. Maybe it's too much. I can't settle down. I can't stop thinking about this TV show *Moonlight* ... it haunts me—it truly haunts me. I don't understand this. I trust, but my question is, 'What good could possibly come out of this?' The intensity is almost overwhelming."

> *Ah, Little One. We say—"Give into your passions." We know you do trust. We know that you know We know what's best for you. And if what is best comes in such a pretty pack-*

*age, what's the complaint? Yes, you worry. But not about the lesson to learn but about the way of it. And your perfectly normal reaction to it. Yes, we say normal. This IS normal for you. The intensity of the subject at hand and the processes in which it is presented to you. Please do not be afraid. And, remember, what you do on your own time is what you do—ON YOUR OWN TIME. Take your time and do what you like with it. You are hurting no one and what you learn will be used to help others.*

"But—Vampires."

*Ah, that is the way of it, is it not? Look for the LIGHT. Look for the good. You are not looking for darkness. That is never your way. You are a lightworker and you must find it where you can. We tell you this: This show is VERY instrumental in what is coming next for you. Actually, it's already begun. Enjoy. Indulge. And Learn.*

*You are a very passionate woman. So, whatever stirs your passions will be used to propel you forward. And love and romance get you every time! So enjoy this little diversion (or is it?) and allow it to bring you forward to a place that is so wonderful and beautiful that you will marvel as to how this all came to be.*

*Yes, we're sure. We love you, Little One. GO IN LOVE (with us by your side). Amen.*

Here is a synopsis of the show according to iTunes: "… *Moonlight* stars Alex O'Loughlin … as a Los Angeles private investigator with a dark secret—he's a vampire. Using supernatural abilities to walk in the worlds of both light and shadow, Mick tries to atone for the wrongs of his past while contending with both his adversaries and growing conflict within." I should add that the conflict is due to his growing love for a mortal woman whose life he saved when she was just a child. Without her knowledge, he has watched over her and protected her for more than twenty-two years.

11.07.07

"Okay—am I on the right track with this? *Vampires—A Path to God.*"

> *You most certainly are. You are getting the gist of what is coming to you—the essence, the beauty. There are so many paths to God; isn't it amazing the way some of them appear? You have noticed the obsession of Moonlight fans. And you are right—they are seeing a beauty, a LIGHT in someone, something, usually portrayed as dark and soulless. It's quite obvious Mick St. John is not soulless but we don't have to tell you that. There is no need to stress over this, Little One. Just follow it to its natural conclusion. We rejoice that you have found such energy, such enthusiasm, such interest in something that practically fell into your lap. But you know these things are never accidental. And you are so well known, are you not? We rejoice with you in your "aliveness" and know you will do wonders with this. How exciting for all!!*

> *Relax. Enjoy. Indulge. Learn. And so it goes.*

11.07.07

> *You feel we are not done and that would be correct. YOU have been specially chosen for this particular assignment. As it unfolds, you will understand what is expected from you. You will have no difficulty performing this task. Task—ha ha. You will be loving every minute of this grand gesture to the Divine. Do not be afraid. Do not be wary. We tell you again to—Indulge. Enjoy. And Learn. We tell you over and over. Lap this up like a kitten laps her milk. Savor it. Slurp it. Allow it to nourish you. For this is food you have waited for, for a long time. We appreciate your willingness, more than willingness—your enthusiasm, to work with Us on this. You are so special to Us. We love you so much, Little One, and the aliveness that has come to you is so spectacular to see. It does our "hearts" good. On with it, Little One. The event has commenced! So be it. Us*

11.08.07

*Ah, Little One,*

*We just want to commend you on a job well done. You are really getting into this "assignment." We knew you would give it your all. And it was known you would throw all of your considerable passion behind it. It will take you places you've never dreamed of. Life will be good!*

*Do not concern yourself with the show—just enjoy it and savor it to the fullest. It is all for you, Little One. You will love the direction it takes—never a boring moment! Such love, such action, such deep feelings portrayed. Again, we say ENJOY! INDULGE! And LEARN! There is much more to learn than you imagine at this time. It will keep you busy for a while. Do not rush it, though. Let the truth come through—as it will—and catch it as it flies. Do not worry, you will not lose out. It is there for the taking.*

*Have a great week-end with your granddaughter and your family and let the love shine for all to see and feel.*

*We love you. Again, do not worry about the duration or direction or the things that can hamper this new favorite for you. Allow things to go as they do. It will be fine.*

*ALL FOR ONE. ONE FOR ALL.*

11.09.07

*Enjoy your show tonight (Moonlight). More to come to feed your thirst for wisdom. Yes, Little One, you will do something with this latest passion and it will connect with others. And be fun for you. "Work" should be fun, should it not? And this will most definitely be used to enlighten others. What an amazing format, no? YES. And we say again, it is so perfect for you—tailor made for you. Just right. Do you believe us now?*

*Linda,*

*Remember to always follow your passions. That's when you know you are really ALIVE—no matter what your circumstances are at the time. You are very good at recogniz-*

*ing them. You think you have little patience. But you have much patience—you wait; you continue on not knowing the outcome; and then you accept. You do not give up and walk away. But, really, how does one walk away from a passion—one may need to tweak it a little to make it a better fit. But the passion is there. What one does with it is the gist of the matter.*

So, I decided to stop my worrying, to just Enjoy, Indulge, and Learn. No better advice than that. See, that wasn't so bad, was it?

# MICK ST. JOHN
# A WARRIOR OF LIGHT

How does one convey the influence, the inspiration, that a fictional character can have on one's life? There is so much and so many that go into his or her making. I would like to think that everyone has been touched in some way by something that is nothing, but yet is everything. From the beginning of history, stories—first oral and then written—have been used to convey the life experience. Whether these stories are recounted around bonfires that provide heat and light, or through television screens, or even on a computer monitor is irrelevant. They give a sense of meaning, even of security, to the day to day existence of the teller and the listener. A good story can impact you on levels that go beyond the superficial. That is what happened to me when I began watching *Moonlight*. There is something very special about this story to me, but equally astonishing is how many others have been deeply touched by it. I can't tell you why some stories speak to us more than others. I just feel blessed to have found one that speaks to me in this space and time. A mere story that has opened my heart space so wide I just have to tell you about it. So, pull up a chair, light a fire, and listen with your heart. That's what I've done. It's made all the difference.

I have been trying to make sense of my feelings of extreme connection to a television show and to its main character, *Mick St. John,* a true hero. The fact that our hero is a vampire is not without meaning. People use words like *undead, dark, evil,* and *soulless* for one such as he. But yet, what I see (and apparently many others do also) is such *light* emanating from him via the television that it can sometimes bring me to tears. I am serious about this. There are no words to describe the impact this character has had on me. The question is: How do the writers convey and the actor (Alex O'Loughlin) portray such *light*? The answer is beyond me. Perhaps it's as simple as we see what we're meant to see. Perhaps not. Perhaps there is a certain kind of magic that occurs when everything involved is aligned in a certain way. But I suspect these questions are as irrelevant as are the answers. The fact remains: This character, in this show, has impacted me more than any I can ever remember. I have come to realize that anything that opens up your heart space, opens you up to God, which is Love. So, maybe that is all this is about. All?

I've already recounted my questioning and the answers given to me about the fact of vampires in my life. But I also had questions as to why this particular vampire was affecting me so much. There had to be more than just a pretty package; there was something deep going on here, something spiritual. And, as usual, my questions were answered. As I was reading a new book that had come into my hand, *Life* by Paulo Coehlo, I came across a description that helped me put all of this into perspective and propel me forward. *A warrior of light.* That was it, of course. *Mick St. John* is a *warrior of light.* Regardless of the fact that he is a vampire, he tries to live a life of integrity against the odds, against what others tell him is his very nature. He knows better. He understands what his better nature is. It might help you to know that he is eighty-five years old, but looks thirty; works as a private investigator; gets his blood from the blood bank; and has made it a rule not to hunt women, children, or innocents. No matter what kind of life he has been given (it was not his choice), he knows how he wants to live, how he is meant to live: to do good, to help others, to harm as few as possible. He lives to serve. Wait a minute, doesn't that sound like a good goal for the rest of us? And he is tortured by who and what he is. I hope that he will be able to resolve that issue and accept, and eventually embrace, who he is. He will be an even better servant. I also look forward to the day when he can believe he is deserving of the *love* that surrounds him. Surely the writers can give him that.

*Little One,*

*As you already know, we applaud your sense of connection to this special being. Of course you would feel a sense of connection. You hear his voice in your head. You recognize the integrity with which he lives. You feel the struggles he surmounts. You watch him try to deny himself the one thing that will help him become whole, the love that has been placed in front of him. Love is a gift of the Divine. Everyone needs to feel loved. And love is felt on so many levels, in so many ways. People always try to label love instead of just soaking it up like the rays from the sun. It is life's blood. It is as necessary to survive the human existence as anything.*

*And who says that a fictional character is any less real than anyone else you come in contact with? Think on that. The human dilemma is one fraught with an attempt to deny emotions, feelings, to always be rational—logical. To always choose the path away from the very core that will take you where you need to go in an easier manner, a more direct route. But that is fine. Whatever the path taken, the journey ends in the same place. The journey ends in a place of love. A place that is beyond description, beyond the senses of mere mortals. A place so loving that stories have been told since time began trying to describe it—to realize it—to recreate it and all the while it was there—it is there—all along. Imagine, just imagine, the bravery required to risk all for such love. To be willing to sacrifice everything that seems so important, to trust in the outcome, and know the overriding certainty that such a life will make a difference. A difference to one and all. Just imagine.*

*There have always been morality tales. This is just another one. But it has appeared in exactly the right time and place to affect many. Many, many mediums can be used to promote a message of love and hope. Never turn away from the one that speaks to you. Amen.*

What comes next is something I have wrestled with. I don't know how to say this. I don't want to say this. This is harder than revealing that angels talk to me. It feels more private, more intimate. But, yet, I feel the urge to put it into writing. Because somehow, for whatever reason, I need to say it; not the angels, but me. It's as if I have to own it. So, here it is: I realize now that in *Mick St. John* I recognize a kindred spirit. Me—a kindred spirit to such a beautiful being—a *warrior of light*? How could this be? Let me explain.

Just before I wrote that last paragraph I asked the angels a question. Here it is along with their answer: "Okay. I'm a little uncomfortable with where this is going. Am I really supposed to compare myself with Mick; to put out there that we are kindred spirits; to connect myself to a *warrior of light*? Isn't that presumptuous or boastful?"

> *Silly One,*
>
> *You know exactly what to do without us telling you. You have known where this was leading all along. Is this stranger or more revealing than saying that angels talk to you? What are you thinking? This is just the kind of thing that others want to read about. It gives them hope for an adventurous, loving life. If it can happen to you, why not to them? This book will awaken the Warrior in more than one person. So, don't be afraid to do this, to share this, to claim this. It is your birthright—and you are ready for it.*
>
> *We know this book has taken some unexpected turns, especially the amount of talk about vampires and the intimacy of your feelings and your thoughts. But do not be afraid to share. Take this risk. It will benefit you as well as others. We assure you this is true. Us*

As you will see from the next entry, which was written before this one, *the warrior of light* theme was occurring frequently as this book got underway. It was easy to write about it in the abstract, even concerning me, words that were intellectually understood but not felt. But when I began to connect the dots, to feel my connection to *Mick St. John*, a real hero in every sense of the word, that's when it all took on a new meaning. And the impact shook me to my core. *A warrior of light* is real, not just a catchy phrase—very real—and I was being called to be one. I think you can understand my dismay and my reluctance to talk about this. It feels very personal, very private. But here's to all the other *warriors* out there, just waiting for the signal. *This is it.*

# A WARRIOR OF LIGHT

Many books have impacted me since I first began the awareness of my spiritual journey. They are nourishment for my quest. One that proved to be exceptionally important as I began writing this book was *Life* by *Paulo Coelho*. You might recognize him as the author of *The Alchemist*, an extremely popular book. I love his books and have read most of them. *Life* is a small book, but full of great spiritual wisdom gathered from first-hand knowledge. It contains quotations from most, if not all, of his books. Each quotation touched me deeply, but the ones that were speaking the loudest—shouting—were the ones from *Warrior of the Light.*

That became an important theme for this book—for my life. Of course I had my usual concerns. I am so predictable. What was all of this talk of warriors and the spiritual life? How did this have anything to do with me? How could I be compared to a warrior when I have spent most of my life as a pacifist? The warrior language made me uncomfortable, but the concept was speaking loud and clear: *a warrior of light.*

"Okay. Where do I go with this one?"

> *Little One,*
> *It's not about the language even though language is important. Do you recognize the theme of good and evil? A concept that most understand even though often incorrectly. We are not encouraging you to connect yourself with something violent. We are encouraging you to see the importance*

29

*of this—the fight to the death. The willingness to risk life to follow your path, to dream your dreams, to focus on what you are doing. The art of 'warfare' is not all about hurting, and harming, and maiming. It is being persistent, assured, single-minded about winning. Giving it your all. Knowing that the outcome is of such extreme importance that there is no way you can give less than your all. There is integrity in that. In fighting for what you believe in. There is no violence contained in this teaching; no one need be harmed. It is more an affirmation of your path at this time. The need for vigilance, for self-assurance, for the willingness to lay it all on the line for others as well as yourself. As you have heard before: All for One and One for All. What you do impacts many. Be assured that your 'fight' will be one of peace and beauty and justice. Do not let labels throw you. Look beyond the words for the meanings. And Own them. Live them. Love them. For this is your way. Enjoy the fight!*

Enjoy the fight? I took my copy of *Warrior of the Light* off the shelf and it has remained with me ever since. It has traveled many miles, from room to room and then place to place, resting in my purse. It truly has become a manual for me. Whenever the telling of my story threatens to overwhelm, whenever I am wary of putting so much of me out there, I turn to it for guidance. I inevitably read something that encourages me or soothes me, that helps me pull out my courage and move forward. If there is anything in *Shot Through the Heart* that touches you, that calls to you, then I encourage you to obtain your own copy of *Warrior of the Light.* It will serve you well.

# THE LIGHT

Obviously, an important theme running though these pages is that of *a warrior of light*. I thought it was time to solicit an angelic definition of the very *Light* we're hearing about.

"What is the *Light*?"

> The LIGHT is LOVE. The LIGHT is GOD. The Light is *anything that makes your heart soar, makes your soul sing, connects you with others and THE ONE.*
>
> *There are as many variations of living in the Light as there are souls to reflect it. People are so afraid of the Light. They are afraid they could not possibly be that pure, that innocent, that loving. But mostly it is because they think they are not worthy. They have been told for so long of their faults, of their failings, of what a disappointment they are to God. They have been told for so long that there is no hope for them except when they have been cleansed by death. But we are here to say, "No!"*
>
> *You need wait for nothing. You need not look to others to tell when you are good enough or pure enough or loving enough. You are all you need. God will show you the Light. God will bring forth the Light that resides in you. God will give you all the direction you need.*
>
> *Love is Light. The directions are spilled out in that one simple phrase. Allow yourself to be more loving, to think more loving thoughts. To do more loving deeds. Not because*

*someone tells you "you must." Not because someone else gives you directions.*

*You know how love feels. You know how to reflect it. Worry on it less and perform it more. Let yourself be free to love. No more "Should I do this or should I do that?" Just do it when it feels right, when you feel so compelled you couldn't do anything else. You can't force love—loving actions. They are either there or they aren't. And when they aren't and you THINK they should be, just move on. There are many other ways that will bring you to love, cause you to share, cause you to make the move that is considered loving. You don't need to force the ones that don't come.*

*Also, don't be afraid of being vulnerable. Much can come when those actions are allowed. We do not speak of physical danger but of a deeper, emotional fear. Of letting the Light out there, of opening yourself to a new way of feeling, of sharing, of moving.*

*What we are trying to say is, "Follow your heart." Then you know when to move. This is not a mandate to love. It is a mandate to allow yourself to love. For when you do, the giver and receiver are one. It is all one action. The action of Love.*

*Think on this.*

So, according to this, a *warrior of light* would be *a warrior of love* and *a warrior of God.* I like it!

# *MOVING BEYOND THE PAIN*

For two days I have been attempting to write about a very difficult experience I had in 2003. But the telling of the story was making me increasingly uncomfortable. It finally occurred to me that there was no reason to tell the tale. There was no reason to submit you to the anguish and pain that I felt. There was nothing to be served by surrounding you with the very energy that I try to combat. It was over and done with in the past. The important thing is what I learned from the experience—the very experience I was meant to have. That was the whole point of the exercise.

I came away with two very important concepts. One was that I wouldn't make a very good disciple if I cared more about the opinions of others than accomplishing the task that I was asked to perform. The other one came to me during a time of deep prayer: "*Some people are called to walk on water. You are sometimes called to make waves.*" No kidding! As I think about this, I realize the waves don't have to be of tsunami proportions; sometimes a nice, gentle, soothing wave is all that is needed. Okay, I feel better already.

I will let the angels take this further. I'm sure they have plenty to say on the subject.

> *Dear Little One,*
> *We salute you. We watched your struggle as you tried to put into words such a painful experience. And we danced*

*with joy when you realized there was no need to share the tale. You are about love and light. Not about revenge or seediness. A thought well thought. A job well done. And we encourage all who read this to understand the deeper message. Let the past go. Let the pain and discomfort fade into the ether. What has been done has been done. Let it go. What you have is today, this moment, the now. There is always a new day, a new moment, a new now. Why on earth would you want to bring such unpleasantness into your present, your future? Let it go. Live life well. Be happy. No worries. Such simple words convey such profound meaning. Commit to living a life well lived—full of beauty, and love, and light. No amount of complaining about the past could ever live up to such a present. We salute you again for recognizing this important fact. Now, take it to heart and get on with the writing you have intended to write. Go in Peace. Us*

# *LIVING WITH INTEGRITY*

We probably all have varying beliefs when it comes to why we are here—why we live an earthly life, what its purpose is.

To me, life is all about living in the Light. The goal is allowing, even inviting, increasingly more of the Light into your life so that you eventually become At One with God. Atonement.

We can take small steps toward that goal every day merely by living with integrity. I see integrity as walking your own path, walking your talk, living your beliefs. I believe our spiritual paths are God given. They are unique and perfect for each one of us, and God has taken into account every aspect of our lives—past, present, and future.

One of the things I am attempting to show with this chronicle is that God *can* use anything as part of your spiritual path. Anything. Chances are that my experiences will be nothing like yours. They are tailor made for me and my life. My goal is to encourage you to open your eyes and open your heart to the path that is laid before you—and try to walk it. That's integrity.

I'm going to let *them* take over.

> *Thank you, Little One,*
> *The way of integrity is The Way. It can be very difficult to live but the rewards are unending. Walking your path, your way, is one of the most difficult things you will do. It is believing in yourself, but more importantly it is believing in*

*God. It is believing in your connection to God. It is trusting in God enough to be willing to place one foot in front of the other not knowing where it will lead. It means that when something you have done causes you shame, or embarrassment, or even disgust with yourself, you know that even that has been a part of your path to God—not just the "good" things you do, but the "mean-spirited," the unloving things you have done to others and yourself. We mention yourself because to us you are as beautiful and worthy of your love as anyone else. God values all. God's love is never ending. It is there for you any time you are willing to make the effort to feel it—to let it nourish you and protect you and save you.*

*And if God is Love, then becoming At One with God means becoming At One with Love. Can you imagine anything more Divine? So be it.*

# PREPARATION

Looking back, I realize I was being prepared for what was to come. Perhaps I was preparing myself. Months before I had any inkling that my spiritual path was going to take a turn, subtle changes began to occur. Most of them had to do with my appearance. The first hint was that I replaced my usual silver wire-framed glasses with shiny black plastic. Then I decided to change my naturally curly hairstyle for one that was super-straight and required professional help. I began to wear black nail polish occasionally. But it was Chanel; no one could confuse that with Goth, could they? I was all about high fashion.

I have long believed that life is a costume party, dressing in whatever way expressed my mood for the day. But this new look was becoming more prevalent. I traded in my twin-set sweaters for long damask coats and dark, bold jewelry. I began to wear a large ring on my index finger. I could say that my look changed because of the change of season, the need for darker, warmer clothing. And it wasn't that I had never worn clothing like this before. But something was perceptively different. I could feel it. I was becoming *edgier*.

What was happening? It was as if some part of me was gearing up to play the part—no, to live the part. This was not about role-playing; it was about real life—my life. Was I taking on my interpretation of Mick's style only in a tastefully feminine way? I hope it was tasteful. Was I surrounding myself with armor—becoming the *warrior* without realizing it?

The angels were right; I could hear Mick's voice in my head—words he had uttered on *Moonlight*. Yes, I had watched each episode numerous times. There was nothing sinister about his words. They were beautiful words; loving, caring, compassionate words. Some were humorous but never hurtful.

And in watching the show, it was as if I was connecting with Mick. Please understand, this was not a teenage girl type of crush. I didn't long to become his girlfriend. From the beginning, I've been rooting for him to admit his feelings for his mortal love, Beth. And, though I admired and appreciated the actor (Alex O'Loughlin), it was the character he portrayed that I was drawn to. It was as if I could feel his feelings, empathize with him. I could feel his emotions; his joy, pain, frustration and anguish, and his moments of happiness and hope. It was as if I could understand him. I know of *empaths*—those who can feel the emotions of others. According to *Wikipedia*, an *empath* is "a person with a feeling expanded sensitivity"—but can this occur with a fictional character? How can this be?

I even purchased pictures of the *Moonlight* cast on eBay. Looking back, I realize that I had gone through a similar process years ago when I was becoming acquainted with angels and the Divine Feminine. I had surrounded myself with depictions of angels in various forms, and I had collected statues of goddesses, the Blessed Mother, and even Mary Magdalene (my personal representations of the Divine Feminine). Apparently I need totems to remind me of what it is I am trying to absorb. This was no different. It was the same; only strange, exotic, mysterious.

Again, the question: How could this be? It could be because it was all in preparation for this mission. Did my soul undertake this transformation to help my human part do her job? Who knows? Does it matter? What does matter is that this was all part of the process—of bringing me to this very space and time, writing these very words in this very book for whomever they are meant to be read by. That's all I know. Perhaps the rest will be known in time or maybe we'll just have to take it on faith. Whatever it is, I believe.

*Well said.*

# THE MISSION

I can't help but wonder what and for whom this book is for. For whom do I write these words, the words that are so hard to put on paper; the words, the descriptions that cause me to lower the protective veil, to let others into the deepest, darkest me? It's as if I must bring them out into the light of day. Such glaring light can be very painful, even harmful. That's something I have in common with the vampires in my life. For me, the risk is not one of life and death; it's emotional. How will *you* judge me?

> *Oh, Little One,*
> *You worry too much. You do not need to put these fears on paper. You know you are doing the right thing by opening yourself up to the scrutiny of others. You also know that some will not applaud your words—your very actions in presenting this life of yours that you live. You know that the fear and loathing that is felt by some will not allow them to listen to your words—to feel your words. You know all of this. And still you continue to write. Because you also know, you trust, that these very words are necessary to move things forward—to teach others about the mission. What mission, you ask? The mission to bring love and light back to the planet—back to Planet Earth. Back to this spectacular home to many. For many love their sojourn on Earth and wish to make it an even lovelier place to live, to reside in. This mission will result in lightening up your homeland. It will bring it to a place where many can see the disasters*

*they have wrought by their lack of love, their lack of caring for each other. So, you see, whoever reads your words can be helped along their own path to freedom—to the love and the light of the Divine. We can only applaud you again for being so honest, so forthright, so open to telling things of yourself that you would be quite happy keeping to yourself. That is what makes you such a good warrior. You know what to do and you do it. No, this doesn't all come easily to you. Not at all. But you, you continue to step out of your comfort zone and give—a gift to all. And we salute you with love and compassion in our eyes. Carry on, Sweet One. The baring continues.*

# A GIFT OF LOVE

On September 5, 2002, I had a chance to deliver a gift of love to someone I had never expected to meet, someone who is very special to me. On that date, at precisely the right time, I was asked to deliver words of love and encouragement to the President of the United States, George W. Bush. Of course I never expected to meet him, who would? And when the chance first appeared, I was reluctant to participate.

President Bush was coming to South Bend to speak at a fundraiser for Chris Chocola, who was running for Congress in Indiana's Second District. The President had also volunteered to have his picture taken with some supporters, for a donation, a large donation. It was a fundraiser, after all.

John declared we should have our picture taken with President Bush. I was appalled. It wasn't the money that bothered me; it's just that I am not a picture person, and I was petrified at the thought of meeting the President of the United States. What in the world would I say to him? But John prevailed and the money was sent. It was too late to back out, but I continued to have misgivings. You can imagine my surprise, and additional anxiety, when I was told that I would have an angel message to give to him. What?!

The day before the event I received this message:

> *You are beautiful, Little One. Please remember that as you attend this most eventful evening tomorrow night. It will be a truly blessed one for you and will leave you with stars in your eyes. We love working with you. You are such a joy. We*

41

*wish you would settle yourself more—alas. But, you have come a long, long way—with much further to go. Have a great day and spread your love and joy to those less fortunate. They need you. Did you know that? They really need you in their lives. Be a blessing to them today. Go in Peace and Love.*

What a juxtaposition: giving an angel message to the President and working at a soup kitchen. If one were to label, words like highest and lowest might come to mind. In reality, just two forms of service—two ways of giving love. They're both a part of what makes up my life.

By the morning of the 5th I was petrified. I still didn't have the message. What was I going to say?

Here is the conversion that ensued: "I am so frightened. I hope I say the right thing."

*You will find just the right words and he will understand and they (your words) will bless him. You are a blessing to so many. He is no different—just a man needing approval and guidance and yes, reassurance. You will provide that to him tonight.*

As the time to leave for the event approached, a very familiar predicament began to take place. John was still in surgery and did not know when he would be free. In a doctor's family this is a constant refrain, and obviously the fact that he needed to leave to meet the President was irrelevant at that time. The patient had to come first. However, I must say that John is often over-optimistic when it comes to time, and there are more close calls than I care to remember. Nothing could be done, so Alex (who was attending the dinner) and I left for the venue. Suffice it to say, there were some pretty harrowing moments, with John arriving just as the doors were about to be locked. We were the last donors in line for the photo-op. Only some police and firefighters were behind us. As it turned out, being last in line proved to be a blessing as it gave us a little extra time with the President. Of course.

By the time of the picture taking, I did know what I was supposed to say, and I continued to rehearse it over and over in my mind until it was our turn. I wish I could tell you what it was, but it was a personal message. I can tell you it was a beautiful message filled with love and encouragement. After I had delivered it, he paused, and then he said, "That was the kindest thing you could ever say to me. I pray for that every day." The picture was taken; I don't even remember it. Then the President turned to me again, with tears in his eyes, and said, "Every day that is what I pray for." And then words came out of my mouth I've never really understood. I suspect they came from a place beyond my knowing. "I know, and you do," I replied. At that point, he reached out and pulled me in for a hug. As we were walking away, John said to me, "Way to go. You choked up the President." I couldn't respond; I was too preoccupied with the stars in my eyes.

The next day I received these words:

*Linda dearest,*

*You need to know that you made such an impact on the President. Those were the very words he needed to hear—a fulfillment of his heart's desire. You probably think that so short a time can not make a difference. It can make all the difference in the world. The world is a better place because of your words to the President. You think not? Just remember that the experiences of one affect all others. The President of the United States received words of love and assurance through a human woman but her words echoed the thoughts of the angels and he knew that. He knew very well what she was trying to tell him and he knew that it answered a longing in his heart. She was his special angel. Here he appeared to help others and in the process received an incredible gift himself.... The sad thing is he rarely gets feedback such as you brought to him. He is surrounded by advisers all of the time—but nothing of the quality of the information you gave him. It stirred his soul, it soothed his soul, it gave him peace, and showered him with the love that was intended. Do you think he didn't see the love in your eyes? Do you think he didn't feel it? Of course he did. He knew it was for him and was of a higher quality than much that he receives. And on a soul level. You were not just physical beings. You were soul to soul. And you provided the light that he needed to help him in this most difficult time.*

As it turned out, for all my concern, the picture was wonderful. And you know, you can't put a price on a gift of love.

# THE DALAI LAMA

Recently, I had the pleasure of attending a public speaking by His Holiness the 14th Dalai Lama of Tibet. This was one of those *highlights of life* that you never expect. He came to speak on the campus of Purdue University in West Lafayette, Indiana. As this is where my son, Alex, attends university, he managed to procure tickets for us to attend. Being able to experience this together was a very meaningful mother and son moment. How the Dalai Lama ended up coming to speak at Purdue is still unknown to me. Even the president of the university seemed surprised. They asked. He accepted. I was there. It was as simple as that.

His connection to Indiana University is well known. His brother, Thubten J. Norbu, is a recently retired professor who founded the Tibetan Cultural Center in Bloomington, where Indiana University is located. Founded in 1979, it is the only Tibetan Cultural Center in the United States. It is dedicated to peace, wisdom, justice, and compassion. On the grounds are two stupas, which are sacred Buddhist monuments that represent enlightenment and house relics. Having grown up in southern Indiana, I have had the privilege of visiting the center. It is a very special place, indeed.

During this visit to the United States, the Dalai Lama was awarded the Congressional Gold Medal, our nation's highest civilian honor. This award, and his private visit with President Bush, sparked an international controversy. The Chinese view him as a separatist, who "conceals his secessionist activities under the cloak of religion." His Holiness asserts that what he is seeking is "a meaningful autonomy" for the Tibetan people; that he is not seeking independence from China.

President Bush has met with the Dalai Lama four times and considers him "a great spiritual leader, a man of peace and reconciliation." When defending his meeting with His Holiness, the president remarked that, "Americans cannot look to the plight of the religiously oppressed and close our eyes or turn away." During the presentation of the medal, the president called the Dalai Lama, *"a universal symbol of peace and tolerance, a shepherd to the faithful and keeper of the flame for his people."*

His talk at Purdue was on cultivating happiness and he spoke a great deal about feeling compassion for all—a depth of compassion that goes beyond the level we normally engage in. He also talked about standing up for what you believe in without feeling aggression for the person you disagree with. He didn't say anything I hadn't heard or read before and he chose to speak in English with occasional help from a translator. I didn't want to miss a word and that required me to focus intently the whole time. There were large television screens for those of us who were sitting quite a distance away from the stage. He seemed almost childlike, giggling and fidgeting, sitting cross-legged in his chair and wearing a visor to protect himself from the lights. It was quite a sight!

It was a nice speech, but I was totally unprepared for the impact his presence would have on me. When he walked on stage I began to shake and have cold chills, and tears began to form. I knew that in this man I was seeing the essence of God. To me, it was undeniable, a most amazing experience. I was totally awestruck for the entire program.

The other thing that surprised me was how many differences of opinion I had with him, especially of a political nature—seemingly big differences such as Marxism vs Capitalism. But what I eventually realized was that our opinions are just human preferences. I suspect we want the same outcomes; we just see different ways of accomplishing them. Is it possible that we make such a big deal out of mere preferences, maybe no more serious in the big picture than choosing dark chocolate instead of milk chocolate? I am reminded of *The Butter Battle Book* by Dr. Seuss. Two neighboring groups come to the brink of war because one group, *The Yooks*, eats their bread with the butter-side up and the other group, *The Zooks*, eats their bread with the butter-side down. It's something to think about, isn't it?

The Dalai Lama took some pre-written questions from the audience and I found one of his answers quite compelling. When asked which world leaders had impacted him most, he spoke of his love for President Bush. He said that unlike many leaders, the president shows his real self. He acknowledged that the two of them disagree on foreign policy, especially the Iraq War, but he spoke again of his love for the president. I think that is a wonderful example of moving beyond our human thoughts and beliefs and communicating on the level of the heart—truly heart speak.

Here is what the angels said to me regarding this experience:

> *Yes, Little One,*
>
> *You most definitely had a profound experience; one you will never forget. The talk was nice but it was the spirit inside the man that affected you on such a level. Truly the essence of God is an amazing experience. That you had the 'eyes to see' such a spirit gave you the blessing of a lifetime. What a lifetime of experiences you will have had—a chance to give a gift of love (an angel message) to a president and to share space with such a high holy man. The spiritual experiences just heap one on top of another. And we encourage you to continue to look with such eyes and feel with such a heart. Truly a blessed experience.*

# QUALMS

It shouldn't surprise you that during the creating of this book, I had some feelings of uncertainty and downright fear. The living and the writing were flowing, but the subject matter was giving me pause. I think it's important for you, the reader, to know that giving the spiritual life your best shot is not always an easy thing to do. Fear and concern kick in. I have learned that what is really important is to move forward in spite of the misgivings, to have enough trust to trudge on until the fears still, as they always do. I thought I would give you a couple of examples of just that and also show you how invaluable my guides and protectors have been to this process. It's quite obvious I couldn't have done this without them and I know that full well. This is a total collaboration done with genuine love on all our parts. It is my hope that you can feel that love because, really, that is what this is all about—what everything is all about. *Love.*

"Help. I'm scared. I was just thinking about what people are going to think about my writing about this stuff: *Moonlight,* vampires, Mick St. John, warriors of light. I thought about how old I am and how people will think it's so silly for me to be writing this stuff. I don't know why it hit but I need some moral support."

> *Little One,*
> *Of course we are always available for moral support. You are just having an attack of fear. It is to be expected. You have been working so hard and accomplishing so much. You have taken much pride in your work. The thinking of the*

*finished product has brought you to this place. You need not worry. We are here. We are always here. You have no reason to fear. It will be a quite beautiful book. You will have so much to say. And the subject matter you use will be refreshing to many. It is unique. It is you.*

*You have no idea what will come of this. We understand your misgivings. But they are for naught. For nothing will stop you. You are committed and you will reach the right people in the right time. There is no need to apologize or feel bad for the fearful feelings you are experiencing. They will happen again and again. But most importantly, you will go on with the work, for your trust is great and the excitement is great and your love and passion are great. There is much for you to do so do not worry about anything more tonight. Get your rest and enjoy your tomorrow. There will be much work to do. We love you. Us*

"I don't exactly understand. Why am I supposed to write about my passion for *Moonlight* and Mick St. John? I know there is a reason but I'm not exactly sure what it is. Why will people care? What business is it of theirs—these strangers I'm writing for? I'm not totally sure what the purpose of this book is. Can you speak to these issues—help still my confusion?"

*Oh, Little One,*

*We have been waiting for this one. Of course, you wonder, you ponder, you feel concerned. But you have no need to. This is a book about opening your heart space. You need to write about what makes that happen for you—what is it that opens your heart space? What was it this time that opened you up so much that you KNEW it was time to write again—not just to write but time to write a book after all this time? An opening so large has occurred in you that you couldn't keep quiet if your life depended on it. And perhaps your life does depend on it—the quality of your life—your spiritual life blended with your physical. There is no way to describe the changes that have occurred in this last few months without describing this show and its impact on you. The fact that this show began at just the time you were waking up from a restful nap was no accident. It all works together for the good. So we ask you to relax your concerns, still your fears, and subdue your embarrassment. It will all make sense in the long run, so we ask you to wait and see. Keep on being you. Keep on opening your heart space. What you don't understand is that now, long before the book will be made public, these experiences have already changed you—have made you even more loving and lively. These changes are being noticed every day by those you come in contact with. But we wish for others, who do not even know you, to feel the passion, the love that exudes from you. It can only do good and much good is needed in this world. More love needs to flow than ever before—and can. So you will do your part, no matter the cost to yourself. You are that loving, that grateful, and that willing to serve. We don't expect you to understand everything at this time. We just ask you to keep on loving, keep on writing, and keep on serving. All will be well. We promise. Us*

# DEEPER INTO LOVE

I feel God's love on a daily basis; that is a given. On a few occasions I have experienced a form of love that goes beyond the norm, beyond the dimension that I usually inhabit. A form of love that fills me and surrounds me—an experience of being bathed in love and light. I believe that I have a covenant with the Divine. God shows me love and I agree to recognize it (in whatever way it is presented to me), experience it, take it in, refine it, and then put it back out there in a new form for others. Some of what I intend to share with you could be classified as merely unusual, but others are of the rarest kind. All of these experiences have been used to take me deeper into love.

A few years ago, I told God I was ready to go deeper into love. I had no idea what that would be or how it would come about, but I made a commitment to experience whatever would come my way. After all, I had asked for it. *Ask, and it shall be given to you; Seek and you shall find. (Matthew 7:7)* As usual, it didn't begin in the way I expected. I'm not even sure what I expected, but being taken deeper into love via a very negative and disillusioning experience was not at all what I had in mind. Sweetness and light would have been more like it.

The very first recognizable teaching experience (following my request) came toward the end of 2004. I attended a spirituality conference in Florida. I had attended the previous one in 2002 and I'd had an amazing time, even picking up some new teachers for the next phase of my journey. It was a very fulfilling and spiritually enhancing experience. But the 2004 conference was destined to play a different role in my life. I can't explain why we sometimes have negative experiences; it would take a wiser mind than mine to speak to that. What I can say is that it is important to walk away from every experience having learned something. And, even though sometimes hard to do, to give thanks for the lessons learned. Perhaps my first clue as to what direction we were heading should have been when a woman sitting next to me asked where I was from. When I told her, Indiana, her response was, "They have a lot of Christians there, don't they?" (Uh, yeah. That would include me.) It was like she thought we were a different species. After a few painful experiences within my own spiritual community, I truly expected this group of *New Agers* to be more open. Not exactly. The overriding cause of the negativity appeared to be that the conference occurred the weekend before the presidential election. This seemed to cast a huge shadow over everything that was happening. Honestly, the tension was not only felt, but it seemed to be influencing almost everyone there. Sides were being taken in a place where I expected more tolerance and understanding. Hostility was even emanating from some of the *enlightened* teachers I had come to learn from. I walked away from there thinking what hypocrites they were.

That's when the real learning began—the first evidence I had of being taught how to go deeper into love. My thoughts about hypocrisy were the catalyst. Starting with those, every time I had a negative thought about anyone, I was instantly shown (in my mind's eye) that very trait in myself. Every single time. At first it was disconcerting—downright freaky. Try living your life, thinking your usual thoughts, and being shown how you reflected the negative trait you were being critical of someone else for displaying. However, after a while, I got used to it, laughing and saying, "You're right." I learned that if I want to be more loving, I need to stop being so critical of others and just look to what's going on with me. What business is it of mine to judge someone else? Just working on myself is a full time job!

One of the more surreal experiences I have had occurred at the orthodontist. I was sitting in the waiting room while my son was being examined. I am embarrassed to admit this, but I was looking at a woman, wondering why she had chosen to wear what she did—fashionista that I am. And then time seemed to stand still, literally stand still, and I saw how everyone in that room was connected. It was like a system of arteries was attaching us. I just sat there marveling at what I was seeing and then it was over. But in that instant I had been shown something profound. If we are all connected, and I have no doubt that we are, then how can we treat others in any way except with love? How we treat them is the very way we treat ourselves. *Do unto others as you would have them do unto you.* (*Luke 6:31*)

I love the Sanctuary of my church. To me, it truly is a sacred space. Perhaps that's the reason I have had some amazing experiences there. One Sunday I was going through what felt like a difficult time. There were a lot of changes occurring in my life and I was being taught things that caused me to relinquish some beliefs I would rather have hung onto. I sat there, during the worship service, reflecting on everything I felt I was losing. I was overcome with a tremendous feeling of despair. In that despair I silently uttered these words, "You are taking everything away. Soon there will be nothing left—but love. I was stunned when that came out. But, really, when it comes down to it, what else is there? Love. It's all about love, isn't it?

On an otherwise normal Sunday, I happened to glance over at a woman sitting in the pew in front of me. It's not that she was a stranger to me; she is a friend that I see every week. But this time something out of the ordinary happened. At that moment I was flooded with love. I immediately knew that what I was feeling was the love of the Divine for her. The love that was radiating inside of me took me to the brink of what I could hold as a human being. It was truly an awesome experience. After the service I did my best to describe the experience to her, however, I doubt that I did it justice. There do not seem to be adequate descriptions for such experiences. But I knew that it was important for her to be made aware of how much she is loved by God. I believe that is the reason for the experience and I feel honored to have been the conduit.

On another occasion, I was filled with anger. Even though a committee had made the decision, there were two particular people I mainly held responsible for doing something I strongly disagreed with. This was not something petty; it was life changing for someone I cared about—in my eyes, he was an angel in disguise. I could not understand their reasoning. I did not want to. As I sat in my pew, I could not even bear to look at them. What happened next is not something I wanted at that moment. I wanted to be angry; I was wallowing in it. That was the least I could do for my friend, wasn't it? Suddenly I felt these words,

*"Father, forgive them for they know not what they do."* Then I understood. No matter what I thought, these two believed they were doing the right thing. Whatever the outcome, they had not intended harm to anyone and they were honestly trying to help others. I believe my lesson in this was about forgiveness and recognizing that sometimes there is nothing to be forgiven for.

Perhaps that Sanctuary has the ability to perform some kind of alchemy on me. It appears the deep love that I encounter there is able to transform despair and anger into love and understanding. That's a pretty potent place, wouldn't you say?

The last experience I wish to share is the most difficult. I have debated long and hard whether to include it. It is such a delicate and painful subject and never would I wish to hurt anyone with my words. However, the experience included such love, there is no way that I can leave it out. It all began on a Friday morning. I was preparing for a weekend visit with my son, Mathew, and granddaughter, London, an occurrence I always look forward to. My husband and other son, Alex, were going to join me and we were even including a visit to my mother. It was going to be a lovely weekend. In the blink of an eye, I was transported into a state of total euphoria—a sense of deep spiritual joy beyond anything I had ever experienced before. And even more amazing (Can there be anything more amazing?) was the duration. This experience lasted for hours, encompassing my two and a half hour drive and beyond. It was a beautiful November day in Indiana; the leaves had turned but had not yet fallen. Throughout the entire drive I felt engulfed in beauty, the intensity so full it brought me to tears. I felt at one with everything—even my car. Seriously, it was as if the car and I were connected as we drove.

When I arrived, I learned that a child was dying. Sydney, a beautiful 14 year old, the sister of Mathew's fiancé, Samantha, was dying of cancer. She was not expected to live much longer. And in my euphoric state I could intuit the beauty of even that. I could grasp the bigger picture—that living and dying are all part of the whole experience, and that there is beauty surrounding our death as there is beauty surrounding our birth. She died before the weekend was over.

Please understand that, to me, the death of a child is a terrible tragedy, but yet I knew she was with God, and that has to be the most awesome place. If I could feel just a small portion of the love and beauty that was surrounding her, protecting her, I could only imagine what awaited her as she returned home. If anyone from her family reads these words, I hope they will understand what I am trying to convey: that this lovely child lived and died in the arms of God, that her beauty and the love felt for her is not diminished by death, and that, in reality, there is no death. Love truly conquers all.

Converting these various experiences into words has been nearly impossible. What I hope you will see is the pattern. Although different in form, with each of these experiences I was taken deeper into love, and came out being more loving myself.

> *Little One,*
>
> *You are very fortunate to have had such an experience of death. One that is experienced by very few. Perhaps the fact that you had never met the child helped you to be unbiased. But you knew of her and you have strong feelings when it comes to children. No one likes to see a child die, an experience to be dreaded by most parents. But do not diminish the response that you had. It was a true and valid mystical experience and one to be valued above many. There is such love awaiting those who depart the earthly realm. This needs to be acknowledged and taught. Death seems such a mystery to most and horrific to contemplate. But it is as much a part of life as is birth and all of the experiences in between. That is a fact. The beauty of each soul is undeniable and their experiences upon returning to the fold is not to be diminished and should be celebrated. But we understand that is too difficult for the loss is just too great. So be sensitive to the pain surrounding the death of loved ones, all the while knowing of the grand reunion that is taking place on the other side.*
>
> *As to the rest of your experiences described on these pages—savor them. As you know, they are rare and of the rarest kind. Such beauty is undescribable but we thank you for trying. Those with ears to hear ... It is important to put this information out there—for others. For the joyous and*

*beauteous descriptions of the sensory form are essential to any good book on spirituality. This is not an experience to be hidden away but shouted from the rooftops. What more evidence does one need than such an experience? How can naysayers possibly describe away the reality of it happening? This is a book about love, about love in its purest form, about how such love is used to maintain connection. And you have done as good a job as any of putting such experiences into words. Let this be. You have done fine. All is well. Us*

I thought with the angel commentary I had put this entry to rest. But still my discomfort over the writing of Sydney's death was nagging at me. Was I doing the right thing including it? As I was trying to work through this, Alex said, "I didn't know Mathew gave you one of Sydney's bracelets." He had seen it on the bulletin board. And then it hit me; in my preoccupation with the writing itself, I had totally forgotten the bracelet—the green rubber bracelet with Sydney's name on it. Mathew had given it to me a few days before. When he handed it to me, he told me to put it on my bulletin board and suggested she might inspire me. Inspire me—perhaps she did. Is it possible that Sydney gave her blessing to the writing of these words? I can't say but I hope it's true.

# THE PROPHECY

What's a good epic without a prophecy thrown in (an accurate one, of course)? I was going to call this entry *Predictions* but *Prophecy* sounds cooler, (doesn't it?) and more fitting to the material at hand.

Lest you think I don't take this manifestation seriously, I do. But, in general, one must try to handle this a little lightly; otherwise you can get lost in the drama. And drama can drag you down, even drain you. I wish I could say I take the predictions I get, write them down, share them with someone, and then put them aside until later, giving very little thought to them. But, in truth, they are hard for me to deal with. You see, I still struggle with what people will think of me. That is probably my hardest fight—to just let things be and not stress over the outcome. Of course I should know better. I know I should know better. And therein lies the rub.

In the last few years, most of my angelic predictions have been related to something that is going on with me or with someone in my family. They have been used to soothe, calm, and reassure during a serious illness and an impending divorce. The truth is, those are much too personal to put on these pages, but I have one prediction regarding a situation that was so public it was a top news story for quite a while.

## *The Elizabeth Smart Kidnapping*

On June 5, 2002, the country was shocked by the kidnapping of a beautiful young lady from her Salt Lake City, Utah home. As time went on, there seemed to be no way to find her and the most reasonable expectation was that she was dead. However, her wonderful Mormon family refused to give up hope, and their faith and trust in God was an incredible inspiration to the rest of us.

On July 4, 2002, I began receiving a message. As you can see, I was not too thrilled about receiving it. Here is what I wrote: "Ok—I'm going to write this but I feel very weird about this. It is definitely a risk for me to write this down."

> *Elizabeth Smart is alive. She will be found. A definite plan gone awry. These people are not murderers. They had no intention of killing her. You must trust this, Linda. You must trust Us. We will help you to understand we are trustworthy and real. There is so much to this story. Look beyond the obvious.*

"What will I do if this is wrong?"
> *It is not wrong. You must trust this.*

Later:
> *Put it aside if you like. Then, when the outcome occurs you will know. You will have written proof. We are glad you shared with Alex. He is a good choice. No need to open yourself to anyone else unless you choose to. But you will have written proof—proof of your ability—proof of your connection to Us—proof of your trust—for you also know we are right. But wait it out—not worrying. What is the worst that can happen—a mistake, that's all. You've had so much verification, confirmation of your abilities and our trustworthiness. Do not let one slip (in your perception, perhaps) stall you or cause you anguish. Please be uplifted. We have given you a gift. Cherish it and use it wisely. We love you, Little One. Again, do not fret over this. Put it aside, let it evolve and see what the outcome is. Remember—we love you. We are here to serve you as you are here to serve others and God Himself/Herself. Please realize this is about Service on all sides. And TRUST.*

At some point I told John of this. Most, if not all, of the experts thought she was dead. That was the obvious explanation, but my angels told me to look beyond the obvious.

And so I put it aside. Elizabeth Smart was found alive over nine months later on March 12, 2003. I still remember the announcement vividly. John and I were watching the news when the story broke. We were stunned. I actually began jumping up and down! Ironically, John had forgotten that I had been given this prediction, but I had not forgotten. And I had one more reason to trust.

# THE TURNING POINT

One day, almost exactly a month into the writing, I reached a turning point. It was the day I realized how much fun I was having writing this book. It stopped feeling like a labor of love and became a gift of love—to me. All of a sudden, it no longer mattered who read the book or what they thought of it or me. I was seriously enjoying this: the writing, yes, but also the living of it. I was enjoying the whole process. My life had taken on a new brightness. It's not that it was not already well lit, but more like going from position two to position three on a three-way light bulb. The light power had been upped. I have to tell you, when your light power is upped, everything around you looks brighter. Nothing has really changed, but everything looks brighter, lovelier, more alive.

I love the fact that God knows us so well, and that anything can be used to remind us of God's love. To me, learning about *love* and *light* through vampires is beyond cool. But if you don't think so—no worries. It's not likely it will happen to you that way. Unless, of course, you're touched by something in this book. Hmm.

> *Oh, Little One,*
> *Dare we say? You've reached a new high. You've reached a point and said words that we've longed to hear. We are not naïve to think you will have no more struggles nor indecisions nor concerns but you most definitely have reached a turning point. And we applaud and we clap with glee. For you understand the importance of this book. You understand that the pleasure in the doing will make the book all*

*that much better—all the more profound. For as the book is written, you are growing. Big time. Do not be ashamed of who you are and what you do. You are a beautiful warrior of light. One that shines light into the darkest spaces. And instead of a sword, you use a pen. Words of light and love that will change hearts and souls. That is what you are capable of and we have seen it all along. We thank you for having such trust in us and the mission that you lived with the concerns not really understanding where we were leading you. Not really understanding the purpose. Just trusting and living and loving. It's all part of the process. Now the book will be finished in record time and the fun has just begun. Trust us on this also. Make way for the glorious future that awaits you. One filled with love and light and fun and adventure and peace and joy and.... Us*

# THE COMING
# OF THE LIGHT

Today seems like the perfect day to write about the coming of the Light. It is December 21, 2007. There are many differing religious celebrations centered around this theme. Most of the great religions, as well as lesser known religions, have special holidays at this time of year. I have learned that the very word holiday stems from the root words, *holy day*. As a practicing Christian I am eagerly awaiting Christmas, but I also confess to an affinity with the Winter Solstice, which begins tomorrow morning at 1:08AM. These two sacred days represent the coming of the Light both figuratively and literally. Obviously, in Christianity, the coming of the Light signifies the birth of Jesus the Christ—the Light coming into the darkness of the world. No one knows the exact date when Jesus was born, but December 25th seems like the perfect time to celebrate his birth. For those of us who live in the Northern Hemisphere, it makes an especially potent recognition; literally, the darkest days are behind us and we have begun the ascent into increasingly longer and brighter days.

Many of our Christmas traditions have evolved from other celebrations, both from ancient times and varied landscapes. For some, that is a problem, but I feel that our *borrowed* traditions add depth and richness to our ways of celebrating. It seems *the powers that be* recognized what was sacred to a people and found ways of blending, which added to the blessedness of the occasion. The Christmas greenery I cherish was originally used to bring the essence of summer, of life, to the dark days of winter. The legend of Santa Claus was based on the life of a saint. What a melting pot of traditions we have. Don't you just *love* it?

I have connected the dots and believe it is no accident that I am writing this book at this time—a book about the Light—not only the coming of the Light, but about recognizing the Light that already exists. Maybe this synchronicity only has meaning for me, and that's enough. But if I needed confirmation, John, Alex and I have been asked to light the advent and Christ candles during the Christmas Eve service at our church. I view this as a very sacred experience and feel honored to have been asked. It seems like a fitting and timely complement to the writing I'm doing.

> *Oh, Blessed One,*
>
> *What a beautiful verse you have produced. Love and light spill from its essence. We have a few more words to add to your prose. You have captured the essence of the light in such a bright way. We wish to speak of darkness. Throughout history and before, darkness was seen as something to fear, something to avoid. The search for light had a much more significant role than in this time when light is so easily had. We think the bounteous examples of light are now taken for granted. But picture darkness, pure darkness—with only the light of the sun to illuminate it. And then picture the warmth from the sun—warmth in truth and warmth in essence. The sun and the moon illuminated the skies at certain times. And those times were cherished beyond imagining at this time. It is true; no wonder these very real manifestations were worshipped. Try to imagine. Now think about darkness. There is nothing inherently wrong with darkness. It is the other side of the same coin. Front and back, back and front. It makes no difference. There is no one without the other. They are both valuable and life giving. Picture the intense heat of a day when you long for twilight and then darkness to cool the air, to cool the earth—the shade you can escape to for a brief respite from the sun. Picture the need for darkness to preserve the very life of plants that depend on the sun for warmth and*

*growth. But too much sun and they wilt and die. Again, light and dark are both necessary for life. We wish in this instant to instruct you and your readers to appreciate the dark, to value the dark as much as the light. They are the yin and the yang of the life you embrace. Embrace both sides of these very life preserving manifestations. Do not fear either but embrace them both with courage and love.*

# OUT WITH THE OLD—
# IN WITH THE NEW

Today is January 1, 2008. Obviously, for many of us, it is the beginning of a new year. In our minds, a new year contains a fresh start, a new chance, an opportunity to begin again. But do we ever really lose what has become important to us in the past? Or do those important moments and important relationships remain with us even as we seem to travel away from them?

Last night I was walking to the beach in Naples, Florida, to view the annual New Year's Eve fireworks with my family. It has become a special tradition for us and a very symbolic way of saying goodbye to the old year, while also inviting the new year in with a *bang*. Literally.

As we became one with the crowd of people heading our way, and trying to avoid the cars which were searching for that elusive available parking place, I had the following insight. It's certainly not an original thought; it has been written about through the ages. However, its impact on me was profound because in that instant I understood it. I knew it beyond the thinking of thoughts, beyond mere intellectual speculation. It became a part of my inner knowledge—a part of my being. What I realized is that all of the people, places, and things that we love become a part of us—of who we are. The love we feel for them actually changes us. A part of our being truly moves, resettles, and we become even more than we were before. All of the seeming platitudes are right. It would be totally impossible to lose those relationships. In an almost magical way, they have contributed to who we are and, in essence, they have become us.

Perhaps for some this makes starting *fresh* more palatable; like a nomad we carry with us what is important. Maybe we don't even need tangible reminders of what has come before. We, ourselves, contain the very evidence of our past.

I was going to say that now the angels will put in their two cents worth, but that would be ridiculous. We all know that their wisdom is beyond price and that perhaps the most valuable of gifts is free for the taking.

*Little One,*

*We commend you on this New Year's Day for explaining your insights so well. You are correct; this truth has been described though the ages and the experience has been sought by many. You have seen it, felt it, become it in just a short time—a short walk—but a walk into the future. On the plane where the past and the future met in the present. A talk of the ages but yet truly available to be experienced now. It is Love that makes you who you are. Yes, dislike and hatred do affect one but they do not become a part of one's being. Only love holds that special place. For Love is who you are. Every single one of you. Everything that exists is there because of love. Of the love the creator holds for the created. Do not misunderstand this important point. It is love that makes the world go round. It is love that sets the world into motion. Do not let anyone tell you that it is anything less than that. Love. All is Love. God is Love. All for One. One for All. Love contributes to Life—your life. And you need not even recognize love for what it is for its presence to be felt—to make a difference. You humans try so hard to control your feelings, to analyze, even to exploit but we just laugh. You can't control love any more than you can control the moon and the stars—and, trust us, even with your greatest scientific breakthroughs, you can not control the moon and the stars! Perhaps the best move would be to allow love in all of its manifestations and treasure those feelings and experiences. Now you do control what you do. Sometimes the choices of what to do are clear and some-*

*times not. When you begin to actually live your integrity, the choices seem easier—not choices at all but imperative. You can do nothing else. But do not be afraid of the feelings. Every gift of love has a reason behind it. You may not know it; you do not even need to know it. But walk the path of love with trust not fear. And know that the you such love is contributing to is the best possible you. Love NEVER detracts or subtracts. Love always enhances and adds to. It is a beautiful world where love resides. Visit it more often. Amen.*

# GOD KNOWS YOUR
# HEART

I often think we are arrogant and elitist when it comes to God. It's not always about going to the mountaintop to communicate with the Divine. It can be, of course, but not necessary—unless it is. God can, and does, find you wherever you are. I promise. We worry so much about the proper way of communicating that we miss out on all the lovely conversations we could have—the heart to heart talks about what some would call nonsense. I do not believe God considers anything about us to be nonsense. We are *the beloved*.

In the entry *Out with the Old—In with the New,* you might have thought such wisdom was provoked by what is considered deep and profound thoughts. Not so. I was thinking about television—about two television shows in particular. One, *Blood Ties,* had been in my life for only a few weeks; its season was done and there were doubts about it returning for a second season. Upon discovering the show, I was able to purchase every episode on iTunes and watch it back to back, several episodes a day. Hey, come on; it's research! I don't even know yet what importance it plays in my life—only that it does. The other show was *Moonlight.* Because of the screenwriters' strike, only 10 episodes had aired, with just two more completed and no concrete information about its future. I was thinking about these shows and the characters in them, and how much they had impacted me and my life, even my spiritual life. I was thinking about my concerns regarding their fate and how the lack of them would affect me—to have found something so special, only to lose it so soon. There was nothing seemingly holy about those thoughts, but the wisdom that came in response was most definitely of a higher kind: *all of the people, places, and things that we love become a part of us.*

There is another example I'd like to share. As some of you know, I have worked in a soup kitchen for many years, at least fifteen. It's easy to become prideful about it. One day as I looked out at the diners, I realized I could see God in each of them—not just in words, but literally. That was truly an amazing experience. But the inner words I heard were just as meaningful. *So, you can see God in them. That's easy for you. The day you can see God in the people attending the Junior League Holiday Ball, you've accomplished something.* Please understand, this is not a criticism of the Junior League or their Holiday Ball. This is just using two extremes as a comparison—one group, often shabby, eating what is considered a humble meal, the other dressed in their finery, eating what is considered to be the delicacies of our culture. For some reason we have been taught the importance of seeing God in one group while the other group has been neglected, at best, and criticized, at worst. But I was guided to look differently, to see the beauty and essence of God in each group, to see that each person is remarkable and made in the image and likeness of God. This opened up my eyes to a whole new world. It's no wonder that the next frontier was something as unusual as vampires; where else could I be taken?

I suppose what I am hoping to convey is that there are no hard and fast rules for communicating with the Divine. We each have our own unique way of relating. The ways of others can be useful tools as we go about finding our way, but they are only tools. They may or may not work for you. It is important that you learn to trust your own way. Also, the network of communication is not stagnant; ways change to fit the circumstances. My best advice is to be open and trusting. If something lifts you up, makes you feel loving—go with it. If something drags you down, makes you feel "creepy" or hateful—walk away. And even if you don't understand the communication, which is often the case, allow it and wait for the meaning to be revealed.

Remember, God knows your heart—knows exactly what information you need and the best possible way to get it to you. Be open and know that a whole new world awaits you, too.

*Ah, Beloveds of God,*

*Yes, God does know your heart—every finite particle and every infinite speck of your being. And while you reside in this life you call "living on earth," the lines of communication remain open. Open to the Divine—open back to the Divinely loved. You have much to help you as you sojourn through the journey of life—to Oneness. You must trust the feedback as you trust the transmitter. If you trust in your God, how can you discount the information placed at your disposal by the One who Loves All? How can you discount all of the beauty and love that is placed along your path— the crumbs of bread that lead you to the promised land? For all is there for you. No, the life can't be lived for you—it is yours alone. But the living of the life is not without its help—its guidance. It would be folly to send you off on such a journey without all of the love and the help that can be given. That is the way of the Creator to the Created. And as you are all of a piece, you must be there for one another. The love felt by all of you is not to be discounted. You may struggle to remember it at times. You may be so enmeshed in your own drama that you forget, but the connection is always there. You are all there for each other. Picture a world in which that is remembered. Picture a world that resides around love. Picture a world in which the essence of God is seen on every street corner and around every block. Picture such a world of love. You can have that, you know. The love is already there. It is just the eyes that require opening. Resolve to open them—to see the beauty and life that surrounds you—that looks back at you every time you look at someone else. Picture that. What would it look like? And how would you get to a place of such seeing? By listening, of course. Listen to the messages, to the whispers that surround you—proclaiming the love and beauty in your path. Listen to the murmurs of love filled sonnets, of songs that never end, of prose and verse that speak of such love. Listen. Listen. Listen. It is there.*

# THE QUEST

As my education has continued, more vampires have appeared in my life. Three of them have played a prominent role. I do not know why vampires have been used as the medium; I do not need to know. Who am I to question the workings of God? What I do know is that I have learned something important from each of them. In Mick St. John, of *Moonlight*, I have seen integrity, goodness, and a true Light-filled spirit. I have also witnessed the futility of not accepting who you are. Through Edward Cullen, of the *Twilight* series of books for young adults by Stephanie Meyers, I have been reintroduced to chivalry. And in Henry Fitzroy, the illegitimate son of Henry VIII, of *The Blood Books* by Tanya Huff and the *Lifetime* television series, *Blood Ties,* based on those books, I have seen someone totally at ease with who he is and possessing a sense of loyalty that almost seems out of place in our modern world. In addition, for more than four hundred and fifty years, Henry has remained a devout Christian. The way he expresses his devotion has reminded me of the importance of Christian ritual in my life. I love the pomp and circumstance of Christian tradition and have committed to make that an important part of my personal spiritual practice.

All in all, quite a lot to learn in a few short months, wouldn't you say? As you can see, to me, these men are not of a dark variety. Flirting with darkness is not a part of my path. I see them as beacons of light.

*Ah, Little One,*
    *You have succeeded in your quest—in the quest for truth and enlightenment. You have risen to the challenge put forth—to discern what each of the precious lights had to*

teach you. *Integrity, goodness, chivalry, loyalty, belief in one's self, and devotion—all wonderful traits to try to emulate. A job well done in this scavenger hunt of life. You did rise to the challenge but it has been an adventure for you. And we have watched with glee as you managed to take from each what was to be given. You have done well. You have searched with gusto and have recognized the prize. And the reward is a life lived even better than before. You have proven to be a true hero. One that will share what she has found. For you know that trust and service and love are all the name of the game. What you find is to benefit all. Your quest has been under-taken for the benefit of others. That is always the way. True enlightenment does just that. It provides higher quality light to all. You all share in this atmosphere you live in. As one's light burns brighter, all lights are enhanced. That is the truth of it. So a quest is never taken at the behest of just one. The fruits are shared by all. Granted, you have a choice as to what to do with what you have learned. But we know that you will share for you understand the importance of the connection to others and you understand the role that service plays in your life. Tell others—teach others—reassure others—of the importance of their lives. That nothing is lived without mean-ing. That everyone has a share in what each and every one of you does. Teach them to respect their lives and know that each small adventure is just a sojourn of a life well lived. There is no reason to fear—no reason to think that their lives are puny or without meaning. What grander quest than to walk the path that has been placed in front of one? Teach them to listen to their hearts, not to the perceptions of others. Teach them to walk without looking back, knowing that the greater moments are ahead. Teach them to spring forward with each step knowing that God is at hand and there are no burdens that need be carried alone. Help is ever near. And newness is just that; it is nothing to fear. Tell them to become carried away with the excitement and the thrill of the quest. And tell them all they need is trust. You tell them these things. They will listen to you and your voice of experience. Tell them.*

# RENAISSANCE

I really wanted to write about this. If it shows up in print, it means the angels have agreed.

I begin with a question. Is there a spiritual renaissance afoot? I believe there is. I understand that a question like this makes some feel uncomfortable, even threatened, but I don't see that an assertion of such a renaissance need conflict or take away from earlier manifestations. In fact, it is an adding to, a layering on top of the base that we already live with; happenings in the present that make the workings of the Spirit manifest in this time, that make it more real for the modern person.

Some even believe that there are cycles that coordinate with astrological signs. There is one theory that I find fascinating. It refers to three spiritual cycles: 1) the time of the Father which corresponds with Aries and is symbolized by the Ram. In Judaism and Christianity this would be in conjunction with the Old Testament. 2) the time of the Son which corresponds with Pisces and is symbolized by the Fish. Obviously this refers to Jesus the Christ who also directed his disciples to be *"fishers of men."* 3) the time of the Holy Spirit which corresponds with Aquarius and is symbolized by the Water Carrier. This represents the outpouring of the Spirit. The *"dawning of the Age of Aquarius"* is believed to be anytime from 1967 to 2150 depending on the expert. Many of us know these words from *Aquarius*, the hit song from the musical, *Hair: "then peace will guide the planets and love will steer the stars."*

Does this mean anything? I don't know, but I believe I see more and more people focusing on their spiritual life—their connection to God. I hear that we have become less spiritual, but I see much evidence of spirituality in our culture today. As a matter of fact, I am sometimes astounded where it shows up. It may take forms that some would call untraditional, but that does not diminish its presence or its function. I love exploring popular culture; perhaps that comes from my sociology background. And certainly my experiences with angels have caused me to give something a second look more than occasionally. Spirituality shows up in books, movies, and music, but the most amazing of all to me is the evidence of it in television. And it's not always where you expect to find it. Isn't that cool? To me it is. I love the unexpected, to be totally blindsided by God. That's all part of the adventure of life that's lived by the spirit. I often think of Wayne Dyer's assertion that we will see something when we believe it. As for me, I believe.

> *Our Little One,*
>
> *Your question as to the renaissance of such spirituality is a good one. First, let us assure that there has always been a deep spirituality afoot. Next, let us say, in every age there have been those with eyes to see it. The question of whether this is a more spiritual age is irrelevant. The answer is only important in the eye of the beholder. The question that needs to be asked is, "Are you more spiritual than before? Do you feel a deep connection to the Beloved One—to the All That Is?" What name you use is up to you. It is the feelings, the living of the connection, which affirm or even deny the existence. Again, do not concern yourself with the masses in this age or any other. Merely concern yourself as to your own life, your own walk, your own service in the name of the Lord. For you have made Jesus your Lord and Master. That is your choice—your way. Do not look in askance at the beliefs of others. Judging is unimportant. Each must choose his or her own way. And there are many ways. What is the fruit of your walk, of your connection, of your life? That is an important question to ask yourself. Through much of life the question should be put to yourself. Not to some supreme questioner—but to yourself. How do you live? How do you love? How do you serve? And the answer is in the stars.*

In the stars?! Wait a minute. "… *love will steer the stars.*"

# GUILT

Personally, I don't want to write about this. I don't want to give power to such a word. I spent years in therapy trying to deal with it, to negate it. Besides, what place does such a topic have in an epic: a tale of warriors and vampires and God? But it crops up when you least expect it, doesn't it? Today was one of those days. This morning, I attended a board meeting of the First United Methodist Church Soup Kitchen. The main topic, as always, was where to get more financial support. I swear, the way we are able to feed our diners mirrors the biblical story of *the loaves and the fishes*. We never really know where the money will come from, or exactly what food, or how much, will show up for us to work with. But in spite of our concerns, people almost always get fed. We do run out of food, occasionally, when we have unexpected numbers, but that's a rarity.

Following the meeting, one of the members was discussing making phone calls to solicit some donations, and the word *guilt* was used with a twinkle in her eye. I truly enjoy her sense of humor; however, the guilt word gets me every time! My response was automatic; I exclaimed that I *hate* the use of guilt. Obviously, I have strong feelings regarding this subject.

Of course, later that afternoon, I began to feel guilty for my outburst, for my use of the word hate, and for being so vehement in my response. In my opinion, hate is a violent word; one which I am trying to release from my vocabulary, obviously unsuccessfully. And thus the need for some angelic guidance.

*Little One,*
   *Some choose to work with guilt; others choose not to. Who are you to judge the ways of others? Again, you must choose*

81

*to work in the way that works for you. It is a matter of integrity—yours alone. That is what we hope to convey—that there are many ways to arrive at the same destination; that finding the one that works for you is the key. Do not waste your time judging how others express this or even feel about it. Do not even waste time judging yourself and your reaction to the very word, the very concept. It is irrelevant. Don't you see? When you judge yourself in such a way, you are provoking the very emotion that you are trying to escape from. It's fairly humorous, isn't it? The very act of denying, creates. Hmmm. There is more to this statement than meets the eye. The moral is that what you focus on, comes to be. That is the way of it. If something unpleasant shows up, perhaps you can laugh at it. Humor is the way of God, you know. What silliness prevails on Earth. How delightful you all can be when you make something insignificant into such serious subjects. Lighten up, we say. Allow yourself to live, to be, to experience. Allow all of those experiences to enhance your life. But when you do something or say something or feel something that doesn't feel good to you, bid it adieu. If an apology is called for, so be it. But then move on to brighter pastures. There will always be regrets but do not get hung up on them. That is a waste of time and precious energy. Move on and don't look back—unless you do. That's fine too, isn't it?*

I don't mind telling you (actually, I do mind telling you) that the contents of this message was unexpected by me. I really expected them to expound on the *sinfulness* of guilt. *Sin* is another word I detest; I'm not about to ask them to speak to that! However, I know they're right; it's time for the judging to be over—of ourselves and others.

Obviously, the point is for me to live *my* integrity. I believe something freely given (not elicited through guilt) contains more power, that it contains the very energy of love. And that is important to me. Therefore, that is how I need to live. How you choose to live is up to you. End of story.

# MEET ME
# AT THE FORUM

These days, many people complain about the lack of community. I think there are still communities; some have just taken different forms than in the past. Through the magic of the Internet, you can connect with like-minded neighbors all over the world. Yes, there are dangers and yes, you must be careful. But that is true of any connection that is made, whether with the person next door or a stranger from across the sea. I have found one of these communities and it has become a valuable place for me to spend time. It is called a forum, but make no mistake, it is a community.

Early on, my passionate interest in *Moonlight* was not satisfied with just viewing the episodes. I wanted more so I went online. Thanks to *Google,* I found all sorts of sites to visit. Some of the places I visited were online forums dedicated to *Moonlight* and peopled by those who were passionate enough about the show to take part in such a community. I found them fascinating. The only forum I had ever been involved with was one dedicated to luxury designer handbags and that was several years ago. Thankfully, I haven't had to disclose that addiction too deeply.

I began *lurking* on two of them; you do not have to belong to read what's posted, only to respond or start a new thread. I thought about joining in, but felt rather awkward about it. However, the seed had been planted and I received this message:

*Linda,*

*You're on the right track. You are pondering the idea of joining and posting on a forum devoted to your newest passion—Moonlight, writing about Mick as a Warrior of Light. Think about it. Think about how many lives you could touch by just putting such a concept out there. You understand the direction and what to say. You would be putting out there an idea so unexpected, so foreign to many that the impact would be tremendous. Of course, everyone will not agree with you (if you choose to do this) but think how many people you could reach. And this is just a start. You have so much to give, so much of your own Light to share, just imagine the ramifications of this. Plant a seed. That's very often all that's needed. And, occasionally, add a little nourishment. The waters (rain) of LIFE will do the rest. Putting something unexpected but yet felt and understood at a deeper level will raise one's consciousness. We think (no, we know) you can do this and make an impact in a direction that's totally unexpected to you. We say, "Go for it," at your own pace and time, of course. But—this would be a good first step in putting yourself (and your own Light) out there for a new audience. See what good comes of it. After all, what could it hurt? And you are bubbling to share this amazing connection you have with this show. We love you. Have a wonderful day!*

So, with this encouragement, I decided to test the waters. I made the decision to join two forums, but have only posted on one. It's the one where I felt most comfortable and also was small enough to build relationships. It seems I really was looking for a community, and in spite of the anonymity, there is a definite connection between the members. We have laughed together, cried together, and been in awe together. We have vented our frustrations about the writers' strike (all sides are represented), and the lack of new episodes, anxiously awaiting word of a second season. We have been there with compassion for those who have reached the limits of what they could take. Perhaps our greatest joy has been watching *Moonlight* win *Favorite New TV Drama* at the People's Choice Awards and knowing how much our passion and commitment played in the outcome. *Moonlight* has an incredible fan base; acquiring over ten million votes does not happen without a lot of devotion and effort.

One day I decided to take the plunge and discuss my spirituality. I had no clue what would happen, but it is who I am. I was not using anything or making anything up just to fulfill an angelic prophecy. I was just being me. I merely answered a thread that appealed to me. It was: *You know you're addicted to Moonlight when …* "… in the midst of writing a book on spirituality, you begin to write about Vampires as a Path to God. Seriously. True Story." Those were my words. Yes, I knew the angels had foretold some responses, but I didn't see how this would happen. I couldn't imagine that anyone would want to correspond with me. I was wrong. I did receive some responses—not too many—but the ones that appeared were very meaningful. All were unexpected, but some were not surprising. Those were the ones using the words *interesting* and *controversial*—totally accurate IMHO which is *web-speak* for In My Humble Opinion. A couple of responses were very affirming, even to the point of congratulating me for attempting to enlighten others.

However, some took a totally unanticipated direction. They seemed to appear out of nowhere. It was revealed that some very passionate fans were afraid to let their families know they were so captivated with a show about vampires. Why? Because they are Christians. At first I was stunned. These were viewers who totally got the show; they even discussed what a moral character Mick St. John is. They saw his goodness and beauty of spirit.

As I began to think this through, I realized I should have seen this coming. I, myself, cringed when trying to explain that I was writing about vampires in my book on spirituality. I know that we all have such preconceived thoughts and beliefs that we are not altogether open to something being different than expected. We are not really open to God working in mysterious ways. And I mean most of us, myself included. What saddened me was that Christians felt they had to hide something that was impacting them at such levels—turning something precious into a guilty little secret.

I tried to help them—to give them words of encouragement. I told them some of my beliefs, such as: anything that opens up your heart-space opens you up to God which is Love; and how people who love *Moonlight* are sending lots of love, beauty, and light energy into the atmosphere, which can be used to help heal the planet and the people on it.

Hopefully, if any of these people, who started out as strangers and have now become friends, read these words, they will look closely at what is happening to them and realize that something amazing is going on, and they are part of it and it is good. I am grateful for such a community in my life. It has given so much to me. It is my wish to be able to give something back.

# EPILOGUE

So there you have it. A slice of my life that mostly occurred in a few short months. Not long as measured in length of time, but amazingly full when measured in experiences and lessons learned.

In *Blood Ties*, our resident vampire, *Henry Fitzroy*, is a graphic novelist. In one of the episodes he was asked the content of the book he was working on. His response was *"passion, politics, good and evil, technology and magic, and a woman in search of her own destiny."* Wow! As soon as I heard his words, I realized that every one of those themes were included in this book. You might think such a connection strange. But to me, it felt right—a validation, if you will. In the words of *Mick St. John, of Moonlight, "I'm not big on categorizing things into strange and not."* Tell me about it.

> *Well, Little One,*
>
> *You have finished. A chronicle of a segment of your life. Descriptions of the life lived along with our commentaries on the subjects. Are you pleased with the results? You should be. You have made a difference—a difference in the way that others will view their lives. A difference in the quality of life lived by many. You have made them think, question, and perhaps even answer. At the least, you have shaken up their thoughts. At the most, more light has been brought into the world. You know it is the latter. For you have lived this; you have felt the light expanding in your own life and you have observed the sharing of the light with others. You know this is a "difference making experience." Never fear that the work*

*has been substandard or of little consequence. You have no idea who or what will be impacted. Just remember: Every little seed planted grows into something beautiful and fulfills its true nature. Everything put into the world expands. So, trust that because of you, the light grows. And do not think this will be the last of your adventures that you share. Who knows what is ahead for you? We congratulate you on a job very well done. And we thank you for your effort on our behalf. Without you, these words could not be written. So, as a team, we rock! We just have a few more words to share with your audience: Until we meet again. Amen.*

That brings us to the end of this chronicle. I feel a sense of sadness, even loss, at its ending. I have loved the living of it, the writing of it, the sharing of it. It seems rather poetic that the last completed episode of *Moonlight* is airing this week. No one knows when the writers' strike will end and still no word yet as to *Moonlight* being picked up for another season. I believe that it will be, but for now I will have to live with uncertainty. I don't feel that this phase has ended, and I don't exactly know what this has all been about. I am aware that something in me has shifted and that I can never be quite the same. However, endings are always accompanied with beginnings. So, even though I don't know what awaits me, what I do know is that it will be another adventure—something more to learn and hopefully grow from. Knowing that I can embark on such a journey, filled with trust and love, propels me forward with more eagerness than trepidation. When that occurs, I hope we cross paths again. Farewell.

# GLOSSARY

Occasionally a word used, by either the angels or me, has a different meaning than the usual or most common definition. In order to avoid confusion, I have included the meanings we have attached to certain words.

Chronicle—a narrative
Dark—little known or kept hidden from others
Epic—a long series of events characterized by adventure or struggle
Fight—to make a strenuous effort to do, obtain, achieve, or defend something
Grace—in Christianity, the infinite love, mercy, favor, and goodwill shown to humankind by God
Imperative—absolutely necessary or unavoidable
Intuit—to be aware of or know something without having to think about it or learn it
Justice—a fairness or reasonableness, especially in the way people are treated or decisions are made
Lurk—to read messages sent to an online discussion forum without contributing
Mandate—an authoritative command or instruction
Narrative—the art or process of telling a story or giving an account of something
Passionate—expressing intense or overpowering emotion, having a keen enthusiasm or intense desire for something, tending to have strong feelings, especially of love, desire, or enthusiasm
Plane—a level or category of existence

Puny—of inferior size, strength, or significance

Qualm—a sudden feeling of uncertainty or apprehension

Renaissance—a rebirth or revival, for example, of culture, skills, or learning forgotten or previously ignored

Talk—a conversation or exchange of ideas or information between two or more people

Totem—something regarded as a symbol, especially something treated with the kind of respect normally reserved for religious icons

Understand—to interpret something in a particular way, or to infer or deduce a particular meaning from something

Verse—to instruct somebody in something

Yang—the principle of light, heat, motivation, and masculinity in Chinese philosophy that is the counterpart of yin

Yin—the principle of darkness, negativity, and femininity in Chinese philosophy that is the counterpart of yang

# *NOTES*

Please note that in the epigraph (the quote taken from Paulo Coelho's *Warrior of the Light*) I have added the pronoun she. It is important to me that the quote speaks to each gender equally.

The news coverage of the Dalai Lama's visit to the United States was obtained from www.cnn.com/2007/us/10/17/dalai.lama/index.html.

The definitions in the Glossary have come from either *The Encarta World English Dictionary* or *The American Heritage College Dictionary*.

The CBS program *Moonlight* and the fictional character Mick St. John are the property of Silver Pictures Television in association with Warner Bros. Television and CBS.

*Blood Ties* is a Lifetime Television series based on T*he Blood Books* by Tanya Huff. The book copyrights are held by Tanya Huff. Henry Fitzroy is a fictional character in both the books and the television series. Lifetime Television is a division of Lifetime Entertainment Services.

The song *Aquarius* comes from the Broadway musical *Hair*—written by James Rado, Gerome Ragni, and Galt MacDermot.

I have quoted from *WARRIOR OF THE LIGHT* by Paulo Coelho. Copyright © 2003 by Paulo Coehlo. (Perennial edition—an Imprint of HarperCollins*Publishers*)

For more information about Linda Porter or her books, visit <u>www.lindaporteronline.com</u>. There you will find out what's new, be able to purchase books, and contact her directly. Be sure to visit her blog (Linda's Words) where she continues to express herself (sometimes you'll even hear from the angels) on a regular basis.

Be assured, Linda would love to hear from you so drop her a line.

978-0-595-50967-6
0-595-50967-3

Printed in the United States
124160LV00002B/1-108/P